WHAT TO READ IN THE RAIN

D1018983

WHAT TO READ IN THE RAIN
 2011

AN 826 SEATTLE ANTHOLOGY
from

FAMOUS AND
NOT-YET-FAMOUS ADULT AND
YOUNG WRITERS

A publication of 826 Seattle

826 Seattle
8414 Greenwood Ave N.
Seattle, Washington, 98103, USA, Earth, Sol, Via Lactea
www.826seattle.org
206.725.2625

ISBN 0-9779832-7-7

Designed by Justin Allan

Front cover photo by Max R. Jensen, courtesy the Max
R. Jensen estate. The Space Needle was constructed for
the 1962 Century 21 Exposition. It was originally painted
Orbital Olive, Astronaut White, Re-entry Red, and Gal-
axy Gold. It has since been repainted. Back cover photo
courtesy Derrick Coetzee, via public domain.

Printed in Canada by Printcrafters on FSC-certified
Rolland Enviro 100 paper.

Special thanks to Amazon.com for
helping fund this project

ABOUT 826 SEATTLE

8 2 6
SEATTLE

AT 826 SEATTLE we match young people and their volunteer adult mentors in our writing lab, located behind the Greenwood Space Travel Supply Company* where together they inspire, teach, write, edit, learn, rewrite, redraft, tutor, invent, and imagine stories, poems, essays, jokes, songs, plays, comics, blogs, invitations, personal statements, job applications, and recipes. All of our programs and tutoring are free of charge to the youth of Seattle.

In our culture, the ability to communicate effectively in writing opens large doors.

Everybody does better when everybody does better.

* The Greenwood Space Travel Supply Company is the world's foremost purveyor of space travel supplies. If you are a space traveler or know someone who is, please direct them to our Earth store at 8414 Greenwood Avenue North in Seattle's Greenwood neighborhood for their travel needs. Or, if you are like many space travelers and prefer cyberspace shopping, visit our website at www.greenwoodspacetravelsupply.com.

All proceeds from sales at the Earth store and the cyberspace store benefit the work of 826 Seattle, which is a 501(c)3 non-profit.

Equally important, all proceeds from this book benefit the work of 826 Seattle.

TABLE of CONTENTS

FOREWORD

Forecast: DRIZZLE

Forecast: SHOWERS

Forecast: DOWNPOUR

Forecast: CATS AND DOGS

FOREWORD

ADVICE TO ASPIRING WRITERS

by Tom Robbins

826 Seattle Board Member and author of nine novels, including
Fierce Invalids Home From Hot Climates and *Villa Incognito*

READ! READ! READ! To be a good writer, you must first be a good reader.

Write! Write! Write! Write every day without fail, even if it's only for fifteen minutes, even if you've eaten too much candy and have a savage belly ache, even if your grandmother has just fallen out of a third-story window.

Fall in love with language. If you aren't already tight with language, start taking language out on dates and see if a passionate relationship doesn't develop. Remember: **language is not the frosting, it's the cake.**

Challenge each and every sentence: challenge it for lucidity, accuracy, originality, and cadence (people read with their ears as well as their eyes). If it doesn't meet the challenge, work on it until it does.

It is not enough to describe experience. You must also experience description. Rhythmical language and vivid imagery possess a power of effect that is independent from content.

Always compare yourself to the best. Even if you never measure up, it can't help but make you better.

Avoid majoring in creative writing in college. There, you'll be force-fed a lot of rules. Many of them are well-founded, **but** there is only one rule in writing: whatever works, works. The trick is knowing what is working. The best writers know that intuitively. It's actually quite mysterious—and it cannot be taught. It has to be **caught.** You catch it like some tropical disease.

Never be afraid to make a fool of yourself. The farthest out you can go is usually the best place to be. (But pushing the envelope has to come naturally, you can't force it.)

Be patient. Be very patient. Stop worrying about getting published and concentrate on getting better. In other words, focus on the work itself and not on what may or may not eventually happen to it. If the work is good enough, it will take care of itself. There have been many prodigies in music and mathematics, almost none in literature. Be patient, engage in life, and gather experience.

Although you'll certainly benefit from a liberal arts education, you might consider going into nursing. Nurses can find employment anywhere in the world, and can usually set their own hours, so you would have ample time to read and write. Moreover, you'd be involved almost daily in human drama, gathering valuable life experience.

Don't talk too much about your work in progress—you'll talk it away. Let your ideas flow from your mind to the page without exposing them to air. Especially hot air.

Since as a writer you'll be spending a great deal of time alone, you will benefit by learning to appreciate the joys of solitude.

As a writer, your most valuable allies will be 1) your imagination, 2) your curiosity, and 3) your sense of humor. Hold on to these qualities against all odds.

Persist! In my past, there were people who were just as talented as I, maybe more so, but they let themselves become sidetracked along the way: (marriages, children, mortgages, greed, fear, discouragement, etc.). If I succeeded and they did not, it was largely because I persisted.

Writing professionally is work—but it is also **play**. Delicious play. So, above all, have a good time. If you aren't enjoying writing it, you can hardly expect someone else to enjoy reading it. If you don't actually like to write, **love** to write, feel compelled and driven to write, you're probably better off abandoning literary ambition in favor of a more legitimate career.

Bless you—and please know that I wish you the luck I wish myself.

FORECAST: Drizzle

Megan Kelso *does not have a middle name. She has been drawing comics for nineteen years and plans to continue drawing until she is an old, old lady. She has lived in Seattle for most of her life except during a six-and-a-half year stint in New York. When it rains, Megan enjoys wet, windy walks through the woods of Seattle's Madrona neighborhood, down to the lake, and up all the public stairways. Her third book,* Artichoke Tales, *was published by Fantagraphics in June 2010.*

Kodachrome

by Megan Kelso

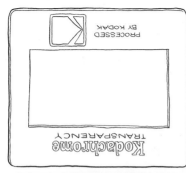

Unbeatable thumb wrestler **John Moe** *is the author of the book* Conservatize Me *and has appeared in numerous humor anthologies. He grew up in the Seattle suburb Federal Way, and currently lives in St. Paul, Minnesota, where he works as a public radio host. To him, rain is just air, really, and he likes to visit the Seattle waterfront in the rain, because contemplating the ocean makes a bit of rain seem like no big deal.*

PRESTO CITY

by John Moe

I GREW UP in the Seattle area. Lived there most of my life. So I know a little Seattle-specific magic trick. Got a minute? Of course you do. You're reading a book, after all.

Okay, now this trick only works if you actually are in the city of Seattle while reading this. Ready? I want you to set down the book and look outside for a bit. Take a good look around, scan the view, take it all in, memorize what you see if at all possible. I will wait here for you.

(Doo de doo de doo, waiting waiting.)

You're back! Hello! Nice place, isn't it? Damp, yes, but it's only water, it's not going to kill you. Same stuff you shower in. You're not made of salt, you're not going to wash away. All right, second part of the trick: Set the book down once more and look around AGAIN.

Totally different city, right? RIGHT? Keep doing it over and over and you'll find the exact same result. Best part of all, it's not even magic. It's just how things are around Seattle. It changes constantly.

Now fine, I admit, the city might have looked mostly the same when you did our little trick there. But trust me, it's different. Because that's the way it works around here. The city is constantly building itself, tearing itself down, building itself up again as something new, getting insecure about that, blowing itself up. It goes on quests to find itself, joins cults, gives all its stuff away, then suddenly goes to law school, graduates and gets a job at a top law firm, then quits one day to start selling hot tubs. That is just who we are.

But it's not always who we were.

I was born in 1968 and grew up in Federal Way, a suburb south about fifteen miles or so. In one of the most spectacular displays of lack of imagination in nomenclature history, Federal Way was named after the federal highway that ran through town, Highway 99. So they called it Federal Way. And that was good enough and it was weird and it would do. It was functional. In my childhood, during the 1970s, Seattle was all about being functional and odd.

It was considered unusual when someone's dad worked somewhere other than Boeing, a place where people built functional airplanes and also sometimes equipment for nuclear missiles, which was a weird thing to do. When I was a kid, a local rock band named Heart started getting famous playing highly functional rock music and they were considered weird because it was two women, and sisters at that. It was probably weird for a lot of people when they rocked harder than just about anyone out there too. Have you listened to "Barracuda" lately? You really should.

But the Seattle of back then knew exactly how weird it really was. There wasn't an Internet to put us in touch with people around the world to whom we could compare ourselves. There wasn't even cable. We were left to our own weird functional devices. It's what I found most enchanting about Seattle. Seattle was a nerd. I empathized.

By the late '80s, people from all over the country started moving here, enchanted by the remoteness and the weirdness and the idea that they could reinvent themselves and get cheap real estate. The result of this influx was that the real estate got a lot more expensive and everyone you met was from somewhere else (usually California). So the Seattle area had been reinvented as a sort of vacation condo that no one ever left. No longer as weird and not nearly as functional.

Soon after that, Seattle got reinvented again when everything got completely weird and totally useless: grunge. See, in my day, we wore flannel shirts because it was cold and they were cheap. We hung out in garages drinking beer because it was too rainy to go outside. We played guitars because it seemed like the best way to impress girls given that we didn't know how to talk to them (thus also the beer, which was cheap because we were poor). We certainly never expected it to be a national phenomenon. So now Seattle had been reinvented as a musical and cultural mecca. What's odd is that even though native Seattleites were fast becoming a minority even then, most of the influential musicians from that era had grown up in Washington or Oregon (except Pearl Jam's Eddie Vedder; he's from California).

When grunge mercifully faded, Seattle was already inventing itself as a tech hub. Sure, we'd had local nerd Bill Gates build up his weird functional enterprise out in Redmond, but other companies started moving in. I went to work for another nerd, Jeff Bezos at Amazon.com. In my three years there, I met one other person who was from the Seattle area. Just one. Everyone else had come to Seattle, looking to reinvent themselves, succeeding in reinventing Seattle again.

Just as grunge had, the tech boom faded and many of the stupider businesses vanished, after briefly reinventing Seattle as a haven for really stupid tech businesses.

After all those reinventions over the years, the Seattle of today—and I say this as a dear friend of the city—is just really screwed up. It's gone nuts. It's a nice place but all that reinvention (not to mention all the shifts before I was born: gold rush, World's Fair, communism) has made it way… jumpier… than Boston, Milwaukee, Indianapolis, or other more stable cities. You take some deep-seated weirdness, add some money, and you get today's Seattle. Buildings get torn down, new ones get rebuilt and then torn down, NBA franchises are taken away for no decent goddamn reason at all (I'm bitter, I went to the 1979 championship celebration), monorail construction projects get initiated and then abandoned. The city changes constantly.

Meanwhile, more and more people are constantly pouring in from all around the world, making it harder to figure out what Seattle is. Frankly, I'm not sure it is even a city anymore. It's like a convention crossed with an airport. Again, I say this as a friend.

A couple of years ago, I got an offer to leave Seattle and move to St. Paul, Minnesota. Not quite as weird as Seattle, highly functional, and much, much more stable. St. Paul has been the same place for as long as anyone can remember. I must admit, it's a bit relaxing living somewhere that isn't constantly trying to define who it is. But it's certainly less exciting than Seattle. I come back to visit Seattle as much as I can and I always feel like I'm landing somewhere new. I look at Seattle when I leave, I look at St. Paul for a while, and when I look back at Seattle, everything has changed. Presto!

Tesla Kawakami *was born in a house she can no longer remember next to a park called Yost. She has lived her whole life in Seattle. Her favorite place in the Pacific Northwest is the beach, where she likes to go out to the sand bar when the tide is low. When it rains, she likes to read the* Little Fur *series by the admirable Isobelle Carmody and make up word games with her friends.*

NORTHWEST BEAUTIES

by *Tesla Kawakami*

EVERY MORNING in the summer I get up and go outside with my not-so-small black notebook and write. I sit on a large wooden chair, which recently fell apart. I love writing outside because I can see my many apple and cherry trees. I can look up and hear the wind, the birds, and the squirrels. When it rains I write inside and even then I watch the leaves dancing underneath the weight of the water.

~ 1 ~

Today it rained and the rain makes me tired. The rain is pretty much all there is in Seattle, but you get used to it. There are a lot of pretty mountains and forests; we're not called The Evergreen State for nothing.

I went on a hike to place called Meadowdale with my friend Tatyana, my Mom, and my dog. The path led to a beach where it was cold, but that was okay. While we were on the walk we saw lots of creeks and rivers, and a tree with branches that dipped down like ladles so you could sit on them. On the tree, I saw a slug crawling and poked him with a stick. He curled into a little ball and fell off, and the stick got really slimy. I put the slime stick in front of my dog's face and guess what? He licked it. Ew.

When I got home I started writing about it. While writing I was hearing the rain and my cat scratching her little house.

After that I went out in the rain and rode my bike around. I found some mushrooms by the big evergreen. My dog was outside too. He picked up his stuffed animal chew toy and waved it in my face. It was really dirty, so I said, "No, Jackie, I can't play with your chew toy, it's too dirty!" So he put it down and started licking it. I laughed and said, "Oh, your Pooh Bear is very clean!"

I came inside and played the piano and drums. My cat doesn't like it when I play the drums because it's so loud, so my mom put my dog's old baby blanket on her. She still looked mad. When I was done drumming I scared her away from her house so I could rearrange things.

~ 2 ~

Today was the day of our school carnival, and it rained! The inflatable slide outside was so wet, the kids who went on it looked like they had a bucket of water spilled on their heads. Luckily, some of the games were inside, so they were not as wet. When we got food we had to rush under a covered spot to eat. Some people were walking around in shorts and t-shirts and they looked like they had been through a shower. I was wearing jeans and a long-sleeved t-shirt.

When it is not raining it is usually windy and/or cloudy. When it's raining really hard and you look outside it gets wrinkly like an old-timey movie. Sometimes I stare at the sky and see the clouds turn into different shapes and I think up stories about them and why they change. I see the clouds turn into many things, like a mouse can turn into a dragon shooting flames from its mouth.

When it's the right time of day and the right time of year, the sky turns beautiful shades of indigo, pink, dark blue, teal, and red. It makes me want to freeze time and stare at it forever.

The birds were calling each other, telling each other to stay away, or calling just because. Some birds sounded high and shrill like moonbeams trying to shine through a dense wood.

~ 3 ~

The sun came out for a while today, which was nice. I was doing my homework outside, sitting on the fence and writing stuff on the fence itself.

I like taking apart grass and looking to see if there is any grass seed in it. The grass seed looks wet, soft, and pale green. It's also very small and light. Laurel bushes, after they flower, grow this weird avocado-ish thing. It's about the size of a penny. Little trees grow in the strangest places, next to garbage cans, in driveways, anywhere.

There is a weed I am starting to see more of. The top has little flower buds but I have not yet seen blossoms. The buds remind me of broccoli at the very top. The stem is long and greenish purple. At the top of the leaf, it looks like a

Christmas tree or an arrow. The middle section is a spiky rectangle and the end is wavy like the ocean. I have seen it grow near gravel and in woodpiles.

On one of the weeds, I saw that spit bugs had laid their eggs. I uncovered some of their spit with a twig and I saw the actual baby bugs. They were orange and about the size of ladybugs. They looked like they might have wings. One spit bug tried to bury itself again so I smoothed the spit back with the twig.

In the spring, I see little green sprouts pushing through the leaves on the ground. This makes me believe you should always try things even if you are scared or intimidated. Chances are, if you know you can do it, you will.

~ 4 ~

Today it was very beautiful because it was sunny. After all that rain it felt like emerging out of a dark tunnel that you had been travelling in for several days. When the sun shoots down rays of light it's like a black-and-white movie was suddenly dipped in a bucket of paint. The colors are so bright and vibrant it's almost blinding.

Seattle has lots of rain, but when it is all over and it gets sunny again, it is so amazing that it makes you appreciate the sun so much more than if you were in other places.

Jess Walter *lives with his family in Spokane, Washington, is the author of five novels, and was a National Book Award finalist in 2006. Two unique things about him: 1. He lived on a cattle ranch as a kid. 2. He hated it. He loves being outside in the rain, but he is not an umbrella person. When it's raining, he prefers to be on Lake Union where he can listen to rain on water while writing.*

STATISTICAL ABSTRACT FOR MY HOMETOWN, SPOKANE, WASHINGTON

by Jess Walter

1. The population of Spokane, Washington is 195,526. It is the 105th biggest city in the United States.

2. Even before the recession of 2008, 34,000 people in Spokane lived below the poverty line, more than 17 percent of the population, about the same as Washington D.C. The poverty rate is about 11 percent in our wealthier neighbors, Seattle and Portland.

3. Spokane is sometimes called the biggest city between Seattle and Minneapolis, but this is only if you draw a completely straight line and ignore Salt Lake City, Denver, Phoenix, and at least four cities in Texas.

4. This is really just another way of saying nobody much lives in Montana or the Dakotas.

5. On any given day in Spokane, Washington, there are more adult men per capita riding children's BMX bikes than in any other city in the world.

6. I've never been sure where these guys are going on these little bikes, their knees up around their ears as they pedal. They all wear hats: ballcaps in summer, stocking caps in winter. I can never figure out if the bikes belong to their kids or if the grown men have stolen the bikes, or, more likely, if they just prefer little BMX bikes to ten-speeds.

7. My grandfather arrived in Spokane in the 1930s, on a freight train he'd jumped near Fargo. Even he didn't want to live the Dakotas.

8. I was born in Spokane in 1965. Beginning in about 1978, when I was thirteen, I wanted to leave.

9. I'm still here!

10. In 2000 and 2001, the years I most desperately wanted to move out of Spokane, 2,645 illegal aliens were deported by the Spokane office of the U.S. Border Patrol. They were throwing people out of Spokane and I still couldn't leave.

11. In 1978, I had a BMX bike. It didn't have a chain guard, and since I favored bellbottom jeans, my pant-legs were constantly getting snagged, causing me to pitch over the handlebars. My cousin Len stole my BMX bike once, but he pretended he'd just borrowed it without my permission

and later gave it back. Still later, it was stolen for good by an older guy in my neighborhood named Pete. I was in my front yard being lectured by my father for leaving my bike out when I saw Pete go tooling past our house on my bike, a stocking cap on his head, knees up around his ears as he pedaled. I was too scared to say anything. Fear has often overtaken me during such situations. I hated myself for that. Far more than I hated Pete.

12. In 1978, Spokane's biggest employer was Kaiser Aluminum. My dad worked there. Kaiser was bought by a corporate raider and closed in the 1990s and all of the retirees like my dad lost their pensions.

13. Now all of the biggest employers in Spokane are government entities.

14. Technically, I haven't held a job since 1994. This does not make me unique in my hometown.

15. The poorest elementary school in the state of Washington is in Spokane. In fact, it is right behind my house. Ninety-eight percent of its students get free and reduced lunch. I sometimes think about the two percent who don't get free lunch. When I was a kid, we lived for two years on a ranch near Springdale, on the border of the Spokane Indian Reservation. My dad commuted sixty miles each way to the aluminum plant. On the third day of school in 1974, a kid leaned over to me on the bus and said, "What's the deal, Richie, you gonna wear different clothes to school every day?" Because of my dad's

job, we were the only kids in school who didn't get free lunch AND free breakfast. At home, we had Cream of Wheat. At school they had Sugar Pops.

16. Sugar Pops tasted way better than Cream of Wheat. In 1974, my dad got laid off from the aluminum plant and we still didn't qualify for free breakfast. You must have had to be really poor to get Sugar Pops.

17. Now they're called Corn Pops. Who in their right mind would rather eat Corn Pops than Sugar Pops?

18. While it is true that I don't technically have a job and live in a poor neighborhood, I don't mean to make myself sound poor. I do pretty well writing books that seem to get published and movies that, thank God for us all, never seem to get made.

19. In Spokane it doesn't matter where you live, or how big your house is, you're never more than three blocks from a bad neighborhood. I've grown to appreciate this. In a lot of cities, especially Spokane's more affluent neighbors, Seattle and Portland, it can be easier to insulate yourself from poverty; you can live miles from poor people and start to believe that everyone is as well-off as you are.

20. They are not.

21. The median family income in Spokane Washington is $32,000 a year. In Seattle, the median family income is

$57,000 a year. Point: Seattle.

22. However, in Seattle, the median house price is $302,000. In Spokane it is $118,000. Isn't there something basically immoral about a place where a teacher cannot afford to buy a house?

23. Drivers in Spokane spend a total of 1.8 million hours a year stuck in traffic on the freeway. This is an average of 5 hours a year per person. In Seattle, they spend 72 million hours stuck on the freeway, an average of 25 hours per person. That's an entire day. Suck on that, Seattle.

24. What would it take for you to willingly surrender an entire day of your life?

25. This used to be my list of why I didn't like Spokane:

    • It is too poor, too white, and too uneducated; there is not enough ethnic food; it has a boring downtown, no art-house theater, and is too conservative.

    • In the past few years, though, the downtown has been revitalized, art is thriving, and the food has gotten increasingly better. There are twenty-nine Thai, Vietnamese, and sushi restaurants listed in the yellow pages. The art-house theater has reopened, near a food co-op. There are bike paths everywhere and I keep meeting cool, progressive people. Given that it's a gorgeous city with a waterfall at its center, and has great weather and a wealth of outdoors activities, Spokane feels like one of those up-and-coming cities.

26. Still, for the most part, Spokane is still poor, white, and uneducated.

27. My own neighborhood is among the poorest in the state. It has an inordinate number of halfway houses, shelters, group homes, and drug and alcohol rehab centers.

28. When I was a newspaper reporter I once covered a hearing filled with wealthy homeowners vociferously complaining about a group home going into their neighborhood. They were worried about falling property values, rising crime, and having "undesirables" live in their neighborhood. An activist called these people NIMBYs—the acronym for Not In My Back Yard. It was the first time I'd heard this term and I thought he meant NAMBLA—the North American Man/Boy Love Association. This seemed a little weird to me.

29. Our house is near a bus stop and people often walk by on their way to the shelters and group homes. These are most often bedraggled and beaten women carrying babies and followed by children. Often they carry their belongings in ragged old suitcases. Sometimes garbage sacks.

30. Poverty and crime are linked, of course. Spokane is ranked fifty-first among cities for highest crime rate. There are about ten murders a year, and 1,100 violent crimes, almost 12,000 property crimes—theft and bur-

glary, that sort of thing. One year, a police sergeant estimated that 1,000 bikes were stolen.

31. I believe it.

32. One time, at our old house, my wife looked out the window at two in the morning and saw an adult male riding a child's BMX bike and dragging another one. He had trouble doing this so he laid one of the bikes down in the weeds. I called the police and crouched by the window all night, watching as they arrested him when he came back for the second bike. I felt great, like McGruff the crime dog.

33. Another time, before I was married, I had gone for a bike ride and was sitting on my stoop when a guy tried to steal my bike. He just climbed on it and started riding. With me sitting there. I chased him down the block and grabbed the bike and he hopped off. "Sorry," he said, "I thought it was mine."

34. What could I say? "Well... it isn't."

35. The largest number of people I ever saw walking to one of the shelters in my neighborhood was five: a crying woman and her four children, all behind her, like ducklings. I smiled encouragingly at her. It was hot that day. I had the sprinkler on in my front yard and the last duckling stepped into the oscillating water and smiled at me. I don't know why this whole thing made me feel so crappy, but it did.

36. One time, I was watching sports on TV when a guy pounded on our front door and started yelling, "Tiffany! Damn it, Tiffany! Get your ass down here!"

37. I went to the door. The guy was wearing torn jeans and no shirt and a ballcap. He seemed sketchy and twitchy, like a meth user. I said there was no one inside named Tiffany. He said, "I know this is a shelter for women and I know she's here." I insisted it wasn't a shelter, that the place he was looking for was miles away, and that I was going to call the police if he didn't leave.

38. He said he was going to kick my ass. I tried to look tough but I was terrified.

39. My lifetime record in fistfights is zero wins, four losses, and one draw. I used to claim the draw as a win, but my brother, who witnessed that fight, always made this face like... Come on. Really?

40. The shirtless guy looking for Tiffany swore colorfully at me. Then he climbed on a little kid's BMX bike and rode away, his knees up around his ears as he pedaled.

41. Later, when I was sure he was gone, I went to the shelter and knocked on the front door. A woman's voice came from a nearby window. "Yes?" I couldn't see her face. I told her what had happened. She thanked me. I left.

42. For days, I imagined the other things I would say to that jerk. Or I imagined punching him. I felt like I'd not

handled it well, although I can't imagine what I would have done differently.

43. After that, I decided to volunteer at the shelter. I'd always see kids playing behind the high fence and I thought I could play with them or read to them. But I was told they only had a small number of male volunteers because having men around made so many women nervous.

44. Of the 33,000 people living in poverty in Spokane, most are children.

45. Right at the peak of my obnoxious and condescending loathing for my hometown, I rented a houseboat in Seattle for $900 a month so I could pretend I lived there. Around that time I was listening to a guy from Seattle talk about all that was wrong with Spokane and he said that it was too poor and too white and too uneducated and too unsophisticated, and I was nodding in agreement until I realized: wait a minute, he just described me. I am poor and white and uneducated and unsophisticated. And I realized that hating the place you're from is just another kind of self-loathing, and that's when I had this even more sobering thought: was I the kind of snob who hates a place... because it's poor?

46. I think there are only two things you can do with your hometown: look for ways to make it better, or look for another place to live.

47. Last year I volunteered at the low-income school behind my house, tutoring kids who need help with reading. One day I was helping this little boy, Dylan. We read a story together about a cave boy who was frightened by a wolf, but the wolf later saves his life and becomes his friend. Every time I showed up Dylan had the wolf book out to read. I'd say, "You should get another book," and he'd say, "Why should I read another book when this one's so good?" Point: Dylan.

48. One day we talked about what scared us and Dylan told me that he was scared that his brother would kill him. I laughed at the commonalities of all people and told him that brothers just sometimes fight, it wasn't anything to be afraid of, his brother loved him, and he said, "No, my brother really tried to kill me. He choked me and I passed out and my stepfather had to tear him off of me. I was in the hospital. He still says he's gonna kill me one day." I reported this to the teacher, who said the boy's brother had indeed tried to kill him.

49. On Halloween, I glanced out the window and saw a woman making her way in front of my house, carrying a toddler. I grabbed the candy bowl, thinking they were trick-or-treating and that's when I noticed a young man walking beside the woman. Out of nowhere, he punched her. She swerved sideways, but kept limping down the street. I dropped the candy and ran outside. "Hey!" I yelled. "Leave her alone!" Now I could see the woman was crying, carrying crutches in one hand and the three-year-old boy in the other. Her boyfriend was

red with anger and he yelled at her. "Your mom told me you were coming here! Now stop! I just wanna talk to you! You can't do this!" I stepped between them. "Leave her alone!" I said. The guy shot back, "That ain't happenin'," but during all of this he refused to look at me, as if I weren't even there. His hands were balled up into fists. His eyes were red and bleary. I was terrified. I told him he just needed to go home. He wouldn't acknowledge me. He kept stepping to the side to get an angle to punch his girlfriend. I kept stepping in front of him. Without a word, the woman handed me her crutches so she could get a better hold of her child. She limped heavily, bravely. This is my hometown, I thought, mine. We air-danced down the block this way, painfully slowly: her, me, him. "Look, I'm gonna call the cops and this is all gonna get worse," I said to the young man. His face went white and suddenly he took a short, compact swing. At himself. It sounded like a gunshot, the sound of his fist hitting his own face. Just then, my neighbor, Mike, came outside. Mike is a big, strapping Vietnam veteran, stoic and easy-going, but about as tough and as reasonable a man as I know. The woman's boyfriend seemed worried by Mike, certainly more than he'd been by me. We stood on either side of the woman. Her angry young boyfriend stalked off. Twice more he punched himself in the face as he walked. He was sobbing. We waited until he was gone and then we escorted the limping woman the rest of the way to the shelter. As we walked, the little boy stared at me. I didn't know what to say. For some reason I asked if he was going trick-or-treating later that night. His mother looked at me like I was crazy. We arrived on the street in front of the shelter and I gave her back her crutches. Mike and I stayed on the street. Because that was as far as we could take the woman. And maybe as far as we wanted to go.

50. The woman knocked on the door. It opened slowly. Mike and I stood there on the street. A gentle hand took the woman's arm and she and her boy were led carefully inside.

Mia Russell *was born July 25, 1996. She loves to write fairy tales. She also loves to read about them.*

NORTHWEST FAIRIES

FROM *826 Seattle Writes The Rain*

by Mia Russell

EVERY NIGHT, when few people are awake, when the sun goes down and the moon and the stars come up, something, some things are stirring, awakening from a deep sleep. All around, they jump from all the corners of the Pacific Northwest. You cannot see them. You can only hear them, but if you believe enough, you too can see them, as I do. Here is a tale of the fairies of the Northwest.

When you hear the word fairy, you think of beauty, sparkles, and joy. But most of the fairies of the Northwest are mischievous and naughty, much like the kids in the Northwest. The last unbreakable spell is one that you can only break when the troll is awake.

Fairies are smart. They're the only ones who know when the troll's awake. So they have you give them objects in exchange for your life.

Not all fairies are mischievous. Some are kind and sweet. They follow a person they have an interest in, and when the person wants something, they do their best to make it happen.

It's the same with the mischievous fairies, too. They follow you and make your life miserable.

You can never tell if they're following you. But they switch off so one day you could have a bad fairy. Then you could have a good fairy following you.

They don't really mean any harm, the bad fairies. They just want to have some fun. And the good fairies don't always do the right thing, either.

THE DRAGONS IN THE SUNSET

Every time the sun comes up and the sun goes down, something is helping it. The reason you can't see is because once they are done helping, they turn into the colors of the sunset.

Don't you ever wonder where the color of the sunset comes from? Yeah, there is some scientific explanation, but did you ever think of the Northwest Dragons?

Dragons from all over the Northwest come in different colors and different sizes. The bigger they are, and the more colors they have, affects the colors of the sunset.

The older dragons have fur, but the younger dragons have nothing but scales. All the same details as the older dragons, but no fur.

Dragons can only change the color of the sunset at an advanced age, and they have to be covered with fur, because their scales are just gray.

The younger dragons do the night sky to get experience for the sunset when they're older.

A lot of the time, younger dragons try to sneak along to help work the sunset. But as they say, one bad apple can ruin the whole barrel. That's how you get bad sunsets.

ODD ELVES

Elves are some of the most magical creatures ever. But they don't use their magic much, because they are very dormant creatures. Their hats represent the wilderness of where they live. It records the waterfalls and streams, which are seen on elves' hats.

Elves are hard workers and spend most of their time working on their homes till they die. Other elves just move into the house where elves die, so they don't hurt a lot of environments.

Tawny Case *is a self-proclaimed nerd, and enjoys read-ing, thinking, not thinking, and making dumb jokes. Also, she knows how to fly… like a nerd.*

WHAT LIES ON DUCK ISLE

FROM *826 Seattle Writes The Rain*

by Tawny Case

YOUR CLOTHES ARE SOGGY, it's true, but rest assured, that is the least of your problems. You didn't really expect Green Lake's oldest legend to be easy to figure out, did you? No, Duck Island remains an enigma shrouded in mystery and wrapped in a puzzle, through its eerie looks and myths that are whispered in the night as joggers circle the lake endlessly, sometimes with a puppy.

After swimming the short distance where your feet do not touch the bottom, you once again feel the silty floor of the lake, and wade slowly towards your quarry: Duck Island. Mind the traps set to defend the isle from intruders! The first layer of defense draws closer as you gape into the water, wondering what traps a lake could set on its own.

Just as you decide you needn't fear, something grabs hold of your ankle! It's a slimy, cold tendril, climbing up, up towards your chest. Now you can see it, your captor, as it winds its way towards your neck—seaweed. You feel it constricting slowly, pulsing with its own freakish beat. Don't struggle; stay calm. It feeds on fear, the fear of drowning, the fear of having a fish touch you, the fear of the high dive, and the slow, creeping fear that slides through you as you approach the rope marking the end of the swim area and contemplate what lies beyond. Stay still, think of ice cream and the puppies that are gamboling at this very moment all around the lake (seriously, is somebody renting them?), and pluck the green vines one by one from your body, until the weed slithers back into the murk, and you continue on your way.

Now you come to the dense wall of foliage that belies the nature of the task at hand, making it appear more formidable by far. What seems to be an impenetrable wood is actually more of a stripe, a fence if you will, of trees, placed there to intimidate would-be visitors. Glance to your left and you will find a rather shabby, dirty, and illegible sign stuck on a post in the mud. Pay no heed to its message; it will take more than a sign to keep YOU from trespassing. If you hear any quacking, it would be advisable to freeze where you are and make not a sound: the duck spies are hidden but ubiquitous.

Step onto the murky bank of the island and find yourself knee-deep in mud. (You hope.) There's nothing to do about it, so push through the muck and towards the center of the island, where the truth awaits. Watch your step, for the little pats of duck poo are not as innocuous as they seem: each triggers an attack from a flock of angry geese when disturbed. Avoiding the goose traps, make your way into the clearing you see just ahead. As you swat away the last tree branches (was it your imagination, or were they reaching for you?) and step into the bald patch on the island, notice how the mud here has not a single footprint on it. Even the ducks and geese dare not tread here; the spot is too creepy. A large mound in the mud, maybe two feet by four feet, catches your eye. Come closer, if you've the courage...

As you draw nearer, slowly, carefully, notice out of the corner of your eye how the mound appears to breathe, but is stonily still when viewed head on. This is what you sought; this is the very thing the others were after. Now it's yours, you think, if you can manage to pick it up and get out of here. But how to lift it? Do you really want to touch it? Steeling yourself, you draw ever closer, hands shaking slightly. The closer you come, the more agitated the lump seems to get.

Right about now the gushing begins. The lump is trembling now, and for a moment you think it will attack you. Then, unexpectedly, it flips over, turning in the muck. You find yourself face-to-face with two enormous green eyes. Though the creature does not speak, it tells you that it is the spirit of the lake, and that you must answer three questions in order to live. If you answer the first incorrectly, you will be made to believe that you are a water nymph and shall live out your life at lake's bottom. Should you answer the second incorrectly, you shall return to society, but be stark raving mad. An incorrect answer on the third spells an eternity in Davy Jones' locker. You begin to see why nobody ever comes out here, and though you are nervous, you manage to choke out your own question. You ask the lump what you will earn should you answer all the questions correctly. It blinks once, twice, thrice, and then you know. You will be set free, and have at your disposal the musical genius that seems to cling to Seattle like a brisk July fog, plus free puppy rental for life.

The first question begins to form in your mind. Why are Seattleites so pale? Well, you think, that's obvious. Because the sun hates us. When you don't feel like a water nymph, you breathe a sigh of relief. This will be easier than you thought. The next question, the lump warns you with uncanny timing, will be much more difficult. Why don't Seattleites use umbrellas? You think for a moment, pondering. Then you tell the lump in a loud, clear voice, that it is because one is not allowed to, by the very nature of being a Seattleite.

The last and final question comes at you, and you stare at the lump. He can't very well let you leave. The lump rises before you, and you see that he is more gigantic than previously supposed. The lump rises to his full height, and comes crashing down upon you with full force! You are crushed under his enormous bulk.

You were WARNED not to go to that island!

Emily Paulsen *has always been writing. She admires Maggie Stiefvater for her "moving stories." Emily likes to spend her time reading, writing, and crocheting. She has spent her eleven years of life in the greater Seattle area. Her favorite place in the Northwest is near a stream where she and her classmates release Coho salmon every year.*

THE 100 BOXES

by Emily Paulsen

It was a rainy afternoon. I was in my raincoat. Only yesterday we had arrived, and already I missed L.A. But perhaps that would change, though our trip would mean a week without my best friend.

I walked down the block, staring at the waves. They looked icy cold in this weather. The Space Needle towered above most of the buildings. It was as if you were an ant and the Space Needle was a mushroom. The black buildings and smaller sidewalks were different from the large sidewalks and tan buildings in my city, L.A. The air was different in L.A., too. It smelled more like flowers from the many basins of plants in front of the shops. Here it smelled more like sea salt. As I looked up ahead again, I saw a sign that in big, bright, red letters spelled the words Pike Place Market!

The place to walk was packed with early morning shoppers like myself. I passed booth after booth. The fragrance of flowers drifted to me from the many tables on my left. At one booth further down there was a lady with thick black hair and teal eyes selling tepees made from intriguing colors of cotton. They were just a little bit bigger than a small child. Everyone strolled the place as if they lived there. I strolled along reading all the signs so I didn't lose my way. It made me feel a little odd, but I was used to it; the same thing happened in L.A.

People all around were trying to sell richly colored silk scarves and wool with bright hues of green and blue. Hats with many logos were hung up high on racks.

I continued on my way, passing stands with fresh fruit, satchels filled with lavender, and jewelry made from sterling silver. I proceeded through the market in awe.

As I wiggled myself in front of a gathering crowd, I saw fish being thrown from one man to another. The sight was breathtaking. People all around me tried to capture it on film as they threw crab, salmon, and trout across the room. One lady in the booth behind us shouted something like, "If you're just watching the fish, start moving!" I resumed walking once all the fish throwing had ceased.

I traveled my way down a slant that led to a lower level. The scent in the air changed from food to more of the smell you get when you walk into an old house. As I got to the end of the walkway I noticed a small shop called Raven's Nest Treasures. I walked in, captivated.

"Hello, are you looking for anything in particular?" the clerk questioned. He looked stern. His hair was straight and blond. It hung just past his cheekbones.

"Oh, I was just looking around," I replied. My hair was as bushy as a rabbit's tail, nothing like his.

I saw spirit stones, each carved with an animal. I saw buttons and fine pieces of jewelry. Mugs with white Native

American designs stared at me. Just as I was about to turn to leave, I saw four wood boxes, each with different carvings, on a nearby shelf. I picked one up. It had a carving of a salmon underwater. It was just smaller than a jewelry box. I immediately fell in love with it and put it on the counter to purchase it. I reached for my twenty-dollar bill. "I'll take this one," I said to the clerk.

"How was your first day in Seattle?" Margie, my mom, asked. She had a tiny face, but we shared the same bushy hair.

"Well, I bought a wood box at the market. Here, I'll show you," I exclaimed. I skipped into the hotel bedroom, and snatched the box up. A small piece of paper fell out, but I didn't notice. I handed Mom the box.

"Wow, Kendall. This is gorgeous!" my mom shrieked. Just then the door opened and my dad, Todd, walked in from his visit to the Seattle Aquarium.

"Well, hello there Kend—what is that?" my dad asked, focusing his attention onto the box in my mom's hands. "That has to be some rare box from, like, the fifties. Kendall, where on earth did you find this?"

"I got it at the Pike Place Market just down the street for exactly fifteen dollars and forty-two cents," I said. I wondered if the clerk had made the box.

Later that night I was in bed reading a book I found, and I saw the slip of paper that I assumed had fallen out of the wood box. It was folded fragilely into fourths. Slowly, and with great caution, I unfolded the piece of paper. In a tiny scrawl in the center of the page were two words: Space Needle. I would have to research this when I woke up.

Ignoring the slip of paper, I went to sleep. My first full day, and I already had some research to do!

The next morning I got up and peered out the hotel room window. It was still raining cats and dogs. I dressed and wrote a note to my mom and dad telling them where I was going to be, and to not worry too much because I was going to be home by dinner. Both my parents were still in bed, sleeping.

I headed out again into the rain, in my raincoat. I went to the library to see if what my dad thought was true. I opened the door. The library was dim, but perfect for reading. People were all around, reading to children and reading alone. The thickly carpeted red floor went perfectly with the oak bookshelves. I went up to the information desk as a lady with grey hair tied in a tight bun greeted me.

"Hello dear girl, is there anything I can help you find?" asked the lady, who I assumed was the librarian.

"Um, yes," I mumbled in reply, confused why this lady got out of her chair just to help me. The people in Seattle must be rather kind. "I am looking for a book about rare wooden boxes."

"Ah, well, I have the perfect book for you! That subject hasn't been touched here for years," the librarian explained as she led me to the very back where several volumes made of leather rested on a dusty shelf. She picked up the first one and handed it to me. "By the way," she mentioned, "the binding is fragile."

As soon as the librarian checked out the book to me, I raced back in the rain to the hotel. I went up the cobblestone streets to the door of the hotel. Once inside, I went up the elevator to floor seven. I sprinted along the carpeted floor to our room, where I stormed in on my parents eating breakfast. I walked over to my bed and opened the book.

I flipped through page after page, scanning through to find the words Space Needle. After about ten minutes, I found a page titled "The One Hundred Boxes from the Space Needle." I read on to find out more information.

In the 1962 World's Fair, there were one hundred boxes made and given out to the first one hundred people who ate at the top of the Space Needle. Each box had a carving of something unique to Seattle. They included salmon, evergreen trees, the Space Needle, rain, and a building burning down on June 6, 1889 when thirty-two blocks of Seattle were burned to the ground.

"Mom! Dad!" I blurted out. "The box I got at the market, it was from the 1962 World's Fair! The clerk at the shop must have been selling the ones that his family received!"

"Really?" they said, seeming as shocked as I was.

"Yes."

"Well, it looks like you got a treasure to take home with you!" declared my mom, as I smiled wide.

"Yes," I said, "Yes I do! I will have to show the people back home my piece of Seattle's history."

Yasmin Said *wants you to know that she is not an eleven-year-old girl; she is actually a monkey! She has always lived in Seattle, and when she is not in school or at 826 Seattle, she likes to spend her time playing sports. She admires her mommy most out of anyone in her life.*

THE RAIN SURE IS WELL

by Yasmin Said

The rain showers down
As it falls to the ground
With its fresh, tropical smell.
It's a rainy day,
So in you stay.
The rain sure is well.

Staying inside
With nowhere to guide
Your thoughts on this rainy day.
Inside's not so bad,
I would be glad
To keep my boredom away.

Playing "Guess Who"
That's something to do
When you win you want to yell!
"Zach and Cody" you can see
When watching TV.
The rain sure is well.

If you live in the Northwest
Cloudy skies are the best.
It always rains for you.
From October and on,
Waiting for spring to dawn,
And the months when the skies will be blue.

Tim Reilly-Crank *is a karate master. He enjoys gaming, writing, skateboarding, and wearing a see-through green visor like an old-timey banker dude.*

HOW UMBRELLAS WERE
LOST IN SEATTLE

FROM *826 Seattle Writes The Rain*

by Tim Reilly-Crank

BACK IN 1851, Seattle had just recently been founded. Unlike the city we know today, that Seattle was very different. Its streets were not bustling, its buildings not tall, and its people craved adventure.

"You're on!" Garen's confidence seemed to float out of his mouth with the words. He realized his mistake immediately. His mind tried to reach out and snatch the challenge out of the air before it reached the tribesmen.

"It is decided then," stated a tattooed native. "You have one day to collect the water as it falls from the sky, and fill our lake with it." At this decree Garen started to perspire, though it was hardly noticeable on his already soaked face.

"J-just so we're c-clear on this," stuttered Garen, attempting to stall for time. "If I accomplish this task then—"

"We will share with you the secrets of the rain," interrupted the chief. "But if you fail, your people will never again have protection from the gods' tears." The tribe's leader motioned that the conversation was finished. Garen barely caught the chief's final words over the loud noise of the rain: "You have twenty-four hours."

The usually boyish red color of Garen's face was replaced with a sickly white. With no time to spare, Garen sprinted home, almost losing his footing in the slippery mud multiple times. He scrambled to round up anything that could be used to gather rain. Buckets in hand, Garen strategically placed them around his home.

As the sun began to set, all the townspeople could hear were the sobs of Garen. "I have failed you. Please forgive me! I didn't know what I was getting into!" Garen repeated, as if the more he said it, the more blame would be lifted from his shoulders. Soon he felt the comfort that only sleep could bring.

The sun beat down on his face so harshly he knew it was punishing him for his actions. Slowly, Garen got to his feet, and began the laborious task of gathering the half full buckets. His trips back and forth from the lake seemed to take an eternity.

When all the containers had been emptied, Garen looked into the lake to see how close he was to filling it. "The soil is barely damp!" bellowed Garen, hoping the gods would hear him and send some relief. But no such miracle occurred. "The only thing left to do is wait for the tribe to come and tell me the verdict," he stated to himself, as if saying it out loud would calm his racing mind.

Finally, the footsteps of the chief and his bodyguard could be heard. Garen closed his eyes in one final prayer to the gods before his fate was sealed.

"You should not have so readily accepted our challenge," advised the chief. "As we agreed, your descendants will lose all protection from the rain."

Garen dropped to his knees, bowing his head as low as he could. "Please sir!" pleaded Garen, "don't punish everyone for my mistake." Eyes focused on the ground, Garen listened for a response. None came. Garen mustered the courage to look up and saw the two natives standing there, the bodyguard holding an oddly shaped knife in his hand.

"Your jacket," instructed the tattooed man. Garen obliged. Peeling the jacket from his shoulders, he handed it over. With one swift cut, the hood of Garen's jacket floated to the ground. Bowing his head again, Garen reached out for his jacket. Feeling its soft fabric in his fingers, he closed his hand around it. When Garen looked up, the two men were gone.

Returning to his settlement, Garen found that all the women's umbrellas as well as the jackets' hoods had mysteriously disappeared. A cool breeze swept the camp, reassuring Garen that all this commotion would pass in time.

David Guterson *spent his childhood and college years in Seattle, where he taught high school English after graduating from the University of Washington. He is the author of seven books including* Snow Falling On Cedars, *and he was a contributing editor for* Harper's *magazine. His non-fiction work has appeared in* The New York Times, *the* Washington Post *and the* Los Angeles Times. *When it rains, Guterson prefers to stay inside and go to bed.*

WHITE FIRS

by David Guterson

They didn't like wet feet is their epitaph—
Snag klatch of white firs across from the gate,
Down from the bull rock dumped by the stream,
Near where a neighbor re-starts his siphon
With a generator and pump in a van.
Gradually they came to ask against the sky,
Ivy refused them, sticks clashed and dried,
And sometimes I thought they looked like men—
Stolid, accusatory, questioning. They set themselves
Off with their leafless June fretwork, they fell in winter,
Cold with disregard. Those still remaining stood
Among the heaped like final pieces on a chessboard.
We called them piss firs for the stink they exhumed,
Struck with a maul, but they were no good for burning
And held whole ponds—so why were they dropping now?
Not even owls dignified their silhouettes.
They were freight cars on the ground, wrecked.

The last wretch fell in the road Monday morning,
And the UPS man, stopped, explained,
"This thing's in the way. Too heavy to move.
I've put in a call. They're bringing a saw.
They'll clean it up and we'll get through.
All of us have things we have to do."

FORECAST: Showers

Jake Lindsay, *eighteen, this year went from Seat-tle's Wallingford neighborhood to Whitman College in Walla Walla, but still swears by his mama, Paseo's Cuban sandwiches, and playing guitar ("Loudly.") when it rains. About his time as a youth mentor at 826 Seattle? "Year to beat."*

FIFTY DOLLARS

by Jake Lindsay

I WAKE UP, very sweaty—probably because of my early-pubescent night sweats (I hope to be in full-power puberty by next fall). I kick off the blankets, get to the bathroom, and do up my hair with the gel my aunt just got me from the freaky Rite-Aid on Broadway. Of course, I overdo it, because I'm a novice of style, and I always overestimate the hair-to-gel ratio. I wash out my hair in the sink, but the stupid old faucet spurts all over me! My shirt's all wet. I take off the shirt and throw it on the bathroom floor—slop! I trash up my medicine cabinet for my eye drops. I have an extra set of eyelashes that grow into my tear ducts—they mess with my eye muscle reflexes, so I can't cry; thus (which is a word I'm trying to use more often—"thus"—because it's extremely archaic), I have to use eye drops every morning. Sometimes I'll still *want* to cry, but nothing comes out; my eyes just get sore and puffy. Actually, it's so painful it gives me a reason to stop myself from crying—

Where's my other sock? I can't ever find anything in this new old house—

I'll have to mismatch! No, but, wait, that's extremely awesome and Seattle hipster now—mismatching socks—

The deodorant my aunt just got me! There was that *Seinfeld* episode last night about armpit hair B.O. Elaine was very anti-B.O. What if I have B.O. in other places? What if I go to school smelling like poo like those bald pajama guys I always get stuck behind at Starbucks? *God: I love Starbucks.*

But I really need be more anti-mainstream if I want to get popular and start dating Eliza. I will. I can do it. Soon, she will hate Blake and all those guys and love me the way I love her. Shut up! You're late! Right now you need to be anti-B.O., like Elaine—she's so quirky. I lather the deodorant on my armpits, belly, thighs, dab it on my neck. I put on a Superman shirt. Where are my shoes?

- Closet? No.
- Under bed? No.
- Everywhere? No.

I find a pair of Spiderman rain boots. I hook them onto my finger and run around with them WHILE I TRY TO FIND MY BACKPACK, CRAP. WHERE IS IT? MY VALENTINE'S IN THERE.

My aunt watches me while she eats standing up at the kitchen table: "Alex, honey, what do you want for dinner?"

"Fa suppah? I dunno, mate. Perhaps somethin' fresh 'n tendah on the bahbie."

Oh, I totally forgot to mention that I speak Australian in the morning.

She chews and crosses her fingers at me, which is our "just-wait-a-moment-I-don't-want-to-speak-with-my-mouth-full" hand signal. She swallows. "OK. Steak. Your uncle'll make steak," she nods at the living room. My uncle is doing jumping jacks. His limbs move two-at-a-time: legs apart, arms up; legs together, arms down.

- Boots? … On.
- Backpack? Found it.
- Card? Yes.
- Ready? Yes.

Out the door.

I ride my bike to school because I know that biking is good for your butt because it tightens the gluteus maximus (which is one of my favorite terms, by the way) and, soon enough, my butt won't be so flat, but —

Crap! I totally forgot to redo my hair!

I turn around, drop my bike on the sidewalk, go to my bathroom, do up my hair, make my way to the door of the house — there he is again: legs apart, arms up; legs together, arms down — and straddle my bike.

—it won't be so flat, but compact, geometrical, lovely like a Pilates instructor — I can just see it! Eliza will love it. She will say: "Ooh, your butt looks so geometrical! Such an improvement from the flatness! Are you biking?" Yes. She will say that.

I will now specify my school schedule and how it impacts me psychologically: Pre-calculus (blarg); recess: go outside on the steps to eat my string-cheese and apple juice, very quiet, sometimes I'll feed the pigeons; bell (crap!): PE: run my stupid laps; lunch break (double-crap!): meet up with Darcie in the quad (she has dwarfism, thus I might write my college essay about our friendship because I'm a critical thinker); try to avoid Blake; try to find Eliza (but she's always with Blake! How could she even like him? I think she's just attached to that stupid crowd. I bet she hates them all though—all her shallow friends. Stupid basketball players. Their sweat and their showers and their puberty hair—Jesus Christ in the Mouth [oh, and forgot to mention that I used to go to: *Holy Rosary High School*. But I got kicked out for: *Unspeakable Contemplation.*]!); bell (crapcrapcrap!): English 11 (doopie-diddle-do-grammar-dickity-do-da); then Human Biology (with Eliza! I know, we totally take a high school sex-ed class together!); then the end-of-the-day bell (phew!); and here we are, back in the present tense, ready to party on (Wayne!—which is my favorite movie of all time).

Someone taps my shoulder in the hallway. I keep walking, betting it's Blake, that butthole—

"Hey, Alex," oh, it's Eliza! Eliza! She found me on Valentine's Day! Eliza! Oh, those wet dark eyes. Those brown marblish things. Kkhaahh. Be cool, be cool, keep walking with her—"'Sup?" I say.

"Nothing." She looks me square in the eye and breathes and smiles. Oh, those wrinkles. "Pretty heavy day of sex ed, huh?"

Oh, God. We were talking about... oh, God.

"Yeah!" I say. "I guess we have a lot to look forward to in college. Ha ha. With all the sex and you know."

She furrows her brow a little and laughs it off. Stupidstupidstupid.

"I mean, of course," I say, "it probably happens here, too, right? I know, like, Sarah and Blake have already... you know—"

"Agh. There's that whole Sarah thing again. I wish people would stop talking about that. It was a long time ago now. Plus, Blake and I were just starting to go out when it all happened. And, you know," she thinks a second. "Blake," she shakes her head. "You can't really blame Sarah. She was drunk and vulnerable."

Oh my God. Please don't say you get drunk and vulnerable. Please don't say that.

"Have you, like, you know?" I say.

Footsteps behind us. We turn around. It's Blake! Here he comes, here he comes, "Hey, babe," he says in his stupid, croaky man-voice.

"Hey, loser," she smiles.

"Ea-sy! I was just about to be nice to you for a change! I made something for you…"

Oh crap. Crapcrapcrap. Please no. Don't do this. Crap! He pulls out a card from his jacket and gives it to her.

"Aw…" She puts the card in her backpack. "Thanks, Blake!" She pecks his cheek.

He snorts a loogie and swallows it. "Yeah, I didn't want to give you flowers because those are, like, too gay."

He winks at me. I turn my back and clear my throat.

"Say, babe," he says. "Can you come over to Tommy's tonight? We're gonna watch some movies and play Guitar Hero."

"Well…" she breathes out and searches her head for an answer. "Sure, yeah—I think so."

"Perf, babe. Just lemme know."

I turn around.

"Oh, yeah, and," he pulls out his wallet and gives Eliza a bill—whoa, a fifty dollar bill.

"Don't forget," he says to her. "You said you'd still do it, remember?"

"I remember."

He turns to me, smirks, and comes up to my face: "Hey, Lexi! How ya doin', sweetheart?"

He strolls over to his group.

Eliza puts the bill in her back pocket.

"Sorry about that," she breathes out. "What were you saying?"

"Oh. Like. I was just wondering if you've ever, like... done it?"

"With who? You mean, like, with Blake?"

"Well, sure. Anyone."

"Um..."

"You don't have to answer that. I shouldn't have asked."

"No, no. It's okay. I'll answer."

She scratches her forehead.

"I have," she drops her hands to her sides. "I know. It's Blake, though. Since we've been going out, he's kind of just gotten what he wants."

She nods, thinking about what she just said.

"But I'm cool with it," she says. "He has good connections. And money. I can get whatever I want from him—long as I ask him, uh... 'nicely,' I guess. I do what I do to get what I want. Sometimes, though, it feels like I really have to do a lot just to please him." She stares at the ground, thinking.

Oh my Jesus, oh my Jesus.

She looks back up to me.

"That goes nowhere, okay?" she says.

I nod.

She stops a second and scans my face.

Still staring. Like she's looking for… something in it…

But her eyes are softer now.

And now I feel her mind in me and I am flushing because

I'm sure she's noticing that my hair is still a little floppy

from this morning —

"You know!" she snaps out of it. "I've been thinking all day whether I should give someone a Valentine." She sighs. "And I just decided it's you."

And I and I and I andIjustdecidedit'syou.

Oh. My. God. She didn't give one to *Blake*. Oh my God. Oh my God. Thus… thus… she likes *me*! She likes *me*, not Blake. She's just *putting on a show*, liking him to fit in. I knew it. I *knew* she was like me all along.

"E-*liz*-a!" I say.

She giggles. "I take that as a yes?"

I nod!

"Okay. Well. This is gonna seem weird, but now I need to write you something on this card I got. Can you just sit tight while I jot something down?"

I nod!

She rummages through her backpack. Oh, those hands. Those delicate little spider-leg fingers. Those rings. Oh she's so. Oh she's so…

She takes out a card. She takes out a card. "Got something to write with?"

I drop my backpack and trash through it for a pen. "Here!"

She takes the pen and then glances over her shoulder.

Blake's still down the hall with his group. Some girls now, too. She opens the card and attacks it with the pen. Writing furiously, nonstop. Jesus. She must really have something to say. She caps the pen and hands me the card.

"Thanks, Eliza!" I stammer.

"You're welcome. Don't open it here, okay?"

"Okay."

She gazes into my eyes.

I breathe.

She comes forward.

And she.

And she.

And she kisses me right on my mouth and God I always knew the shape of her lips, those tight little pink wedges, but I could never—never—know of how soft…

"OK," she says so close to my face that I can feel its heat. "I'm gonna go."

"Wait a sec. I…"

Jesus. Stop star—

Stop staring at her face, at her mouth, at her eyes, her ears, and just talk.

Just talk.

"I…" I twirl out of my backpack and find my Valentine. "Here."

"Oh…" she looks over her shoulder again. Blake and his group are silent and facing us. "No, you don't have to—"

She freezes and looks at me funny.

Still pausing.

Thinking or something.

Getting awkward.

Getting awkward.

Awkward getting!

"Do you want it?" I try. "I mean, it's cool if you don't..." Stop apologizing you weirdo, she wants it—she kissed you!

"Yeah, yeah. Sorry." She takes the card and scurries over to Blake and his group.

What the **what** was that? Oh, who cares. Who cares! She kissed me. Shekissedme!

I sprint off campus, backpack flapping, runningrunningrunning to the bike cage across the street. My hands tingle. My head floats. The cage is empty. The flag flutters and clinks above me. It's cool out. I feel rain. I feel wind. I look out through the cage to the skyline. The Needle. The everything. This city, this place! This place where people are okay with kids like me. This place where there are so many other Elizas, so many girls. Maybe it's not so bad being away from mom and dad—

The gravel crunches behind me. I turn around. It's Blake! And his group. And...

"Come on, Blake. Let's not do this, OK? I don't need to be here," says Eliza.

"Lexi girl. How's Valentine's?" says Blake.

Oh my God. Oh my God. I turn around and unlock my bike, trying to ignore them, because that's what my aunt says I should do.

"Blake," Eliza swivels in front of him and comes up close to his face. "We're leaving."

"Oh, sure, we'll go. I just think you should give little Lexi here another dyke kiss."

The guys and girls ooh and snigger.

"Nope," Eliza turns to me. "We didn't agree to that.

I'd kiss her once—that was it."

"Ten," says Blake.

"No," says Eliza.

"Twenty."

"No."

"Thirty."

"Go to hell."

"Fifty."

"Go to hell."

"Come on, fifty."

"Damn it, shut up!" she turns back to Blake. "You shouldn't have dragged me into the bike cage, God damn it. Now you're insulting me. All right? Now you're insulting me."

She strides off.

"Eliza!" he calls out.

"You know," she calls back. "I think I'll be on my own tonight."

"Eli—" he stops himself short and clenches his fists. He exhales. He looks down. And then his face shifts to me.

My eyes sting, starting to swell.

Don't cry. Don't cry. Dontcrydontcrydontcry.

Go.

I straddle the bike and hit the pedals and zip straight and fast for a way out but Blake kicks the bike frame and I topple over and get pinned under it.

They circle round me.

"No wonder," Blake clicks his tongue. "No wonder your mom and dad abandoned you to your aunt and uncle.

You worthless dyke. You worthless dyke."

    They walk off.

    Dontcrydontcrydontcry—remember that you're stronger than him.

    I squirm out from under the bike and slump against the wall of the bike cage. I go through my backpack. I breathe. I open Eliza's card.

> *Please.*
> *Will you ever?*
> *Will you ever?*
> *What can I possibly do to say I'm sorry?*

Don't cry.
    Don't cry.

> *Eliza*
> *I'm sorry, but, you're mesmerizing.*
> *I know I'm a girl,*
> *And I know I haven't known you real long,*
> *But I hope you can understand and won't be freaked out.*
> *Happy Valentine's Day.*
> *Alex*

You   worthless dyke,   don't   cry.

Ryan Boudinot *is the author of the novel* Misconception *and the collection of short stories* The Littlest Hitler. *He was the only first-grader ever selected by Conway Grade School to attend Seattle Pacific University's Young Author Conference. That was 1979. Now, at age thirty-seven, his six-year-old son is teaching him to recite all forty-four presidents in order. He appreciates the sound of raindrops hitting maple leaves, and gets grouchy if it's sunny two days in a row.*

DORIS BURN AND THE SUMMERFOLK

by Ryan Boudinot

WHEN I WAS THREE or four years old, my mother enrolled me in an art class at the Mount Vernon YMCA, taught by a wonderful woman named Heidi Epstein. Heidi gently guided us from one activity to another—pipe cleaners and construction paper, tempera paints, beads, Elmer's glue and glitter, googly eyes, crayons, and little pieces of wood. In the name of creative freedom, Heidi let us gravitate toward whatever held our interest most. In my case, that meant an intense period crafting soap dishes with clay. Every class ended with a snack and story time. Heidi's taste in children's books was superb. I came to recognize the seal of the Caldecott award on the covers of many of the books she read to the class, finding her selections better than most of what was being read to me at school.

One afternoon, Heidi read *The Summerfolk*, by a Puget Sound author named Doris Burn. It's the story of Willy Potts, who lives on an island with his dad, a fisherman. Every summer the island is overrun with tourists who raise a ruckus with their speed boats and leave their peanut butter sandwiches in the sand. To escape this invasion, Willy retreats to the swamp behind his house, where he keeps a broken-down row boat and likes to get his head "nice and empty." On the day of the summer solstice, while he's meditating in his boat, Willy feels he is being watched and turns to find a strange boy dressed in a sort of Huck Finn/pirate get-up, watching him from the bank. The boy introduces himself as Fedderly and asks Willy if he'd like to join a flotilla. Willy begrudgingly agrees to follow Fedderly, and finds that his boat is a magnificent sort of do-it-yourself pirate ship. They embark on a trip through the swamp, meeting Rosebud, a reclusive girl living in a thicket of

rosebushes; twins named Cork and Spinner who play in an elaborate complex of tree houses, swings, and nets; and Twyla Loo, a girl who tells spooky tales in a tree house high in the willows. At the end of the story, Willy returns to his landing and bids farewell to his new friends, who disappear into the tule grass. The ending is ambiguous—are these just other "summerfolk" like the tourists who invade Willy's beach, imaginary friends Willy dreamt up, or a tribe of children living independent of the adult world?

I was so enchanted by *The Summerfolk* that I revisited it frequently throughout grade school, and later read it to the kids I "watched" when I became a summer camp counselor. One afternoon at the Mount Vernon public library, I came across another of Doris Burn's books, *Andrew Henry's Meadow*. I recognized the style of illustration immediately and took it to an empty table to savor every page. Andrew Henry is a boy who likes to invent things. His inventions—a helicopter suspended from the ceiling of the family kitchen, a system of pulleys in his little brothers' room—are always

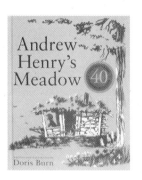

earning him the ire of his family. One day Andrew Henry decides he's had enough, packs a bag of supplies, and heads through a swamp, over a hill, and through the deep woods until he comes to a meadow. Here he builds himself a fort with a special landing strip for dragonflies. Before long, a little girl named Alice Burdock shows up with her birding supplies. Her parents don't appreciate her love of birds, so Andrew Henry builds her a tree house. Several other children arrive, each exiled from the adult world due to their particular interest. One boy loves boats, one girl likes to play dress-up, another girl loves playing music. Andrew Henry builds them each their own little fort, and soon a village has sprung up in the meadow. Inevitably, the children's parents miss them too much and search for them, discovering the meadow and enjoying a joyous reunion. With a new appreciation for Andrew Henry's gifts, his family gives him a corner of the basement where he can tinker and invent. The end.

Willy's and Andrew Henry's surroundings were intimately familiar to me. I grew up on a seven-acre triangle of land in rural Skagit County that included a pasture, fruit trees, two ponds, and several acres of woods that were part of a forest too vast for me to explore in a single childhood. The couple who'd sold the property to my parents had literally used parts of it as a garbage dump. They'd pitched trash down the slope of the hill toward the deeper of our two ponds since at least the 1950s, giving my dad an excavation project that lasted decades. Over the years moss and weeds and small trees had grown over the trash, as if to reclaim the surface of the earth. I spent weekends as an amateur archeologist, unearthing brown glass bleach bottles, rusted whorls of box spring mattresses, the hood of a BMW, silverware, a crusty Gumby doll, cables, small appliances, and pieces of mysterious machines. Across our pasture sat an ancient refrigerated train car with the word "Dairygold" faded on the side. We used the train car as a place to store hay, and I named it my "lab." In my lab I performed experiments with all the weird discoveries I made around the property. Mostly these experiments involved breaking bottles with rocks and turning pipes and cables into traps. I visited my lab every day after school and spent a good part of my weekends there lying in the hay, reading science fiction novels. After a time I didn't visit my lab to create anything so much as to get my head nice and empty like Willy's. The lab became a physical anchor for the creative work I did in my mind, a setting where I enjoyed the freedom to entertain myself and my friends.

Reading Doris Burn's books felt precisely the same as playing in my lab. I knew I shared something with this author, feeling she had tapped that inner state in which I felt most happy, the place where I made up games and imagined myself a hero of a science fiction drama played out among the vine maples and stinging nettles.

In 1998, while I was in graduate school, I sought out copies of *The Summerfolk* and *Andrew Henry's Meadow* online, paying $60 for out of print editions. It dawned on me that Doris Burn might still be living in the Puget Sound area. Wouldn't it be fun to track her down and tell her what her books meant to me as a kid? I found a phone number for a "D Burn" living in Anacortes, but failed to rally the courage to make the call. Years passed. I got jobs, lost jobs, and watched in astonishment as my son Miles was born in January of 2004. In the months leading to his birth I started spending more time in the children's sections of bookstores, building a library in anticipation of his arrival. I bought Sendak's *Where the Wild Things Are*, James Marshall's George and Martha stories, and loads of Dr. Seuss. I mostly looked forward to reading Miles *The Summerfolk*. When Miles was about three years old, I introduced him to the book, curious if my baseball-obsessed son would appreciate the story's sensibility of rural play. Miles loved it, and loved *Andrew Henry's Meadow*, too. Now our everyday conversation is sprinkled with references to the two books, to Alice Burdock and her birds or Cork and Spinner, the tumbling twins passing their days in the Green Alder mansions.

In the spring of 2007, I was working at Amazon.com on the DVD team and was startled to see a movie called *Andrew Henry's Meadow* on a 20th Century Fox release schedule. According to imdb.com, Doris Burn's classic book had been optioned by Zach Braff of *Garden State* fame. I also discovered that *Andrew Henry's Meadow* had been brought back into print by Seattle-based San Juan Publishing, who also planned to bring back *The Summerfolk*. I contacted the publisher, who told me that Doris Burn had just celebrated her 84th birthday and lived on Guemes Island, a seven-minute ferry ride from Anacortes. I decided now was the time to meet her.

Born in 1923, Doris Burn grew up in Portland, Oregon, attending college at Oregon State until a stroke debilitated her father and her family couldn't afford tuition anymore. She moved to Seattle and worked a series of unsatisfying jobs that nonetheless paid the bills and financed an eclectic education at the University of Washington. For a while she worked for the phone company, monotonously reading the time of day aloud every fifteen seconds and asking callers to buy war bonds. Never declaring a major and taking whatever classes interested her, she was allowed to graduate from UW after completing a thesis. She married Bob Burn, the son of Farrar and June Burn, two free spirits who had arrived in the Northwest to homestead in the San Juans in the early twentieth century. Doris and Bob moved to the family homestead on Waldron Island, a spot of land in Puget Sound that remains without electricity or running water to this day.

Waldron was a bohemian community of artists and dreamers where Burn's creativity flourished and where her four children were raised. Even today it's a place with more pianos than television sets. Every Easter, Waldron's residents gathered at 4:00 a.m. at the east side of the island just to witness the sun rise together. There were dances that went so late into the night that the children bedded down on quilts laid beneath the tables and chairs of the dance hall. The children of Waldron were the true stewards of the island's culture; for months they built a scale model Incan village with temples and terraces by the shore. They made sure the adults observed all the holidays they invented and often just wandered through the woods, heading in no particular direction, uncertain where they'd come out. At least two generations of Waldron's children played a game called Boo Hoo. All the participants of Boo Hoo pretended for weeks that they had been abandoned in the wild by their parents and were forced to create their own society. At the game's conclusion, the children were reunited with their parents, upon which they wailed "Boo hoo!" with sadness for losing the little world they had created.* Surrounded by

---

* This playful spirit of childhood animates Waldron to this day. While doing research on the island for this article, I just happened to get back in touch with one of my best friends from high school, a guy named Jason Lillis who spent several months in the mid '90s on Waldron in one of the Burn family cabins. When I asked him about the island culture he told me a story about a night in which he and his girlfriend were sleeping in the cabin and were awoken by heavenly singing around 3 a.m. As the singing grew louder, the stairway began to glow with candlelight. A procession of little girls wearing white robes, each bearing a candle, appeared at the foot of their bed, serenading them, then silently retreated once the song was complete. Jason described it as one of the most beautiful experiences of his life. He soon learned this was a tradition related to one of the child-created holidays of the island.

the island children's boundless imaginations, Doris taught for a time in Waldron's one-room school house, one of the eight schools in Washington state supported by a program to provide education to children in remote areas.

In the late 1950s Burn's marriage to Bob reached a point at which she began contemplating life as a single mother. With no reliable income and hesitant to jump into a full-time teaching career, she borrowed $500 and took her youngest child, Sarah, with her to Seattle, where she purchased a train ticket to New York City for $65. Upon arriving in New York she rented an apartment from her in-laws for $25 a month and set about establishing a career as an illustrator. The best way to do this, she figured, was to find books she thought were illustrated poorly and to illustrate them better. She nervously took these illustrations to editors, walking around the block several times before she mustered the nerve to enter the publishers' offices. She absorbed advice and encouragement and during meetings left Sarah in the care of a European woman next door who admired Doris's devotion to her art. Doris wrote and illustrated a book called *The Horrible Haircut*, and while it has never been published, it was enough to pique the interest of an agent. One editor, noticing how nervous Doris seemed, asked, "You want to know if your illustrations are professional, don't you?" When Doris nodded, the editor said, "Yes, they're professional." Buoyed by the praise, Doris skipped across Washington Square Park. She remembered a question her son Mark had asked years earlier, "Mom, how much would it cost to build a cabin in the woods?" At that moment the idea for *Andrew Henry's Meadow* began to take shape.

According to her About the Author blurb, Doris Burn wrote both *Andrew Henry's Meadow* and *The Summerfolk* on Waldron, hauling enough water to her cabin in the morning to make tea and rinse her brushes. Actually, she drank coffee, not tea, and much of *Andrew Henry's Meadow* was written and illustrated late at night by the light of a kerosene lamp while her children slept. Her books were popular enough to get picked up by the Weekly Reader book club, and *Andrew Henry's Meadow* earned her a Washington State Governor's Award for Best Children's Book. Established as a children's author, she went on to write and illustrate a wild west story called *The Tale of Lazy Lizard Canyon* and illustrate nine more books written by other authors.

By 1977, when *Lazy Lizard* was published, Doris Burn's career in children's books had run its course, and she attended to the demands and joys of her family. One son, Conrad, moved to the Congo with the Peace Corps where today he is establishing a bio-fuel program. Mark, the inspiration for Andrew Henry, moved to Port Townsend and became an inventor, developing, among other things, a new process for freezing fish. Skye and Sarah live in Bellingham and pursue careers in nonprofits and academia. In the early '90s Doris moved to Guemes Island to care for her mother, who passed away at the age of 106. Doris still lives in her mother's home, a few minutes from the passenger ferry from Anacortes. When I arranged over the phone to meet her, I told her I'd be wearing a green jacket. "I'll be the old lady," she said.

I still find the experience of meeting authors for the first time strange and thrilling. How can the stories that populated my head have any relation to the living, breathing world of actual people? But there she was, smiling and waving as I stepped off the passenger ferry on a perfect June afternoon. At her home, she offered me coffee and confided that she always enjoyed hers with a little dollop of ice cream. In modest, neat surroundings with sun streaming through her garden, I told this author whose books had been my childhood's faithful companions what her work meant to me and my son. I was happy to hear I wasn't the first fan to seek her out. One family showed up at her house and recounted how their boys had duplicated every one of Andrew Henry's inventions. And then there was that call from Hollywood.

"When Twentieth Century Fox called it about blew me off the island!" Doris laughed. This is actually the second time *Andrew Henry's Meadow* has been optioned for film. Zach Braff bought the rights after the first option expired, signing on to write the screenplay. During our visit, Doris expressed the concerns of every author whose works are optioned for film, that they do justice to the book. I told her that regardless of how the movie turned out, it would certainly generate interest in her books and ensure they remain in print for years to come. Then I asked if she still had her original manuscripts.

Doris said she kept the manuscripts in a space above her closet, and went to fetch a ladder. I steadied the ladder as she climbed, imagining the news story about how a beloved children's book author fell and hurt herself while retrieving her work for a young writer from Seattle. She pulled down a thin, battered cardboard box that contained the twelve-by-fifteen inch illustrations for *Andrew Henry's Meadow*. They were gorgeous and crisp after forty years, with blank space where the text would be. We spread them on the kitchen table, chuckling and narrating the story together. Here was Andrew Henry with the helicopter in the kitchen, trekking across Worzibsky's swamp, coming to the meadow, building his village. The richly detailed illustrations, particularly those of the outdoors, felt lived in, as though they were drawn from places I used to play. The way Burn draws a shady forest invites you inward; you want to step through those boughs and explore. Alice Burdock poised with a bird perched on her head as Andrew Henry speaks to the boat-loving George Turner communicates such tranquility. These children are comfortable in their skin and happy to just be children. The little homes that sprout up in the meadow are almost inconceivable, just beyond what a gifted eleven-year-old architect might be capable of building. *Andrew Henry's Meadow* and *The Summerfolk* are so compelling this way, rooted in realistic details that nonetheless allude to what children can envision when they just squint a little at their familiar surroundings.

At the end of our visit, Doris asked about my own writing career. I felt shy to say anything about the short stories and novel I've written, humbled in her presence, and proud when she told me I had raised her spirits. Mostly I felt the satisfaction of completing a task some thirty years in the making, expressing my gratitude for her gifts. The stories Doris Burn created by kerosene light in her cabin on Waldron Island remind me of how my imagination once filled a world of unearthed treasures.

Noah Sather *is another self-proclaimed teenage nerd. In his spare time he thinks up monsters and odd gadgets. He is currently working on a gorilla with cat arms.*

THE NORTHWEST MYTHICAL AND UNKNOWN CREATURES ORGANIZATION MEETING #66

FROM *826 Seattle Writes The Rain*

by Noah Sather

"ORDER, ORDER!" yelled the living tree. "May the Northwest Mythical and Unknown Creatures Organization meeting commence! Does anyone have any questions to bring up?"

"Aye, aye, bend thy ears in my direction!" said a large stone troll. "Can thou getteth this poultry to cease messing on my feet? 'Tis a habit most unsatisfying."

"I told you to plug your ears when they play Shakespeare on you. I cannot understand a word you are saying!" exclaimed the tree. "Now, does anyone else have anything to say?"

"I would like to say that you are full of sap," hissed a shadow in the corner.

"That was uncalled for," said the unaffected tree. "And now on to the problems. As this is my cave, I will go first. The loggers are cutting my kind down, so I want the whole of you in the forest tomorrow causing mayhem. Next on the list, and I believe, last, the rain pixies."

"OUR HOME IS BLOCKED BY A MOUNTAIN

OF ACORNS ON THE GROUND, SO WE CANNOT GET IN!" screeched the pixies.

"That is simple enough to fix," said, the tree. "Troll, I want you to... Troll! Have you been drinking coffee again?"

The jittery troll had a large jug of coffee in his hands, was shaking uncontrollably, and was talking very fast. "Tis true my dear fellows, I loveth coffee, I lovethlovethloveth-lovethlovethloveth thy fine and earthy grounds!"

"Okay," the tree said uncomfortably. "Without the troll, I will burrow underneath the nuts with my roots, sinking them into the ground. Orange goo, you eat the nearby squirrels, shadow, you make the place invisible to humans, and the rest of you, hide the acorns that have sunk into the ground with dirt. All right, we will do that Thursday. Meeting adjourned!"

And with that, all the creatures went to get some sleep, for they had much work ahead of them.

The End... or at least until the next meeting.

Emma McIntosh *loves to sing, act, read, and write. While this is her first published work, she hopes it is just the beginning. In fact, she plans to be a professional writer some day. Emma lives near Green Lake.*

EMMA'S HUNDRED-WORD STORIES

FROM *826 Seattle Writes The Rain*

by Emma McIntosh

SAVING SEATTLE

IT WAS A DARK and stormy Northwest night. Katie walked down to the market square. She had to get there before the Others did. She sped up. She was frightened. Who wouldn't be?

Standing by the bronze pig at the entrance to the market, she listened. Ticking. No! The Others had already been here. Think!

Defuse the bomb! HOW?!

She reached into her raincoat pocket and pulled out some gum and hairpins. It might work. She carefully twisted the pig's foot and it came off. Ten seconds: she gummed up the works. Five seconds: removed the timer. The ticking stopped. Sigh. Seattle was safe. For now.

LIGHTNING BEACH

IT WAS A DARK and stormy Northwest night. Jessica walked along the shoreline. The wind and rain whipped her face. Lightning flashed; she could see the ocean. She smiled and headed back to her house. As she walked, something made her turn and look back out to sea. She saw a boat on the water. Who would be sailing on a night like this? The boat was going to crash on the rocks! She tried to signal the boat to no avail. Lightning shone on the boat and on the ghosts aboard her. Knowing she could do nothing, Jessica watched the ghost boat sink.

THE QUESTION AT KING STREET STATION

IT WAS A DARK and stormy Northwest night. This wasn't the most memorable way to do it but this was his last chance! Mark was in the King Street Station waiting for the 12:45 train from Portland. The small box in his jacket pocket felt like it weighed down his whole side. He glanced at his watch—12:46; hordes of people streamed through the double doors. He waited for what seemed like a lifetime and then he saw her. Grace walked into the station, luggage in hand. She spotted him and ran over. They kissed. Then he asked the question.

LEFT OUT IN THE COLD

IT WAS A DARK and stormy Northwest night—but Lidds was used to that. She didn't like being outside in the middle of it though. Jerry should have been home by now to let her in! What was wrong? Traffic? She didn't know. She never would unless he told her and that only happened once or twice a month. Yep, she'd never get anything out of him. Here he comes! Try and look cute.

"Hiya, Lidds! Sorry I'm late, old girl."

Old! Left out in the rain and now he says I'm old!

"Sorry. You're such a good dog, Lidds!"

LUNARA'S SECRET

IT WAS A DARK and stormy Northwest night, and something had just fallen out of the sky. Lunara rolled out of her mangled spacecraft. She hurt all over from her crash landing: She touched her head. Blood. Hippszbac! She was dying in a strange world. She'd never be able to carry out her mission. She would have someone else complete it! But first she needed to rest.

Hank walked to where he saw smoke. He nearly collapsed with shock at the sight that met him. He walked over to the woman and knew he'd never know her secret.

THE DEADLY RENDEZVOUS

IT WAS A DARK and stormy Northwest night. He walked along the observation deck of the Space Needle. This was the perfect place for the rendezvous. The doctor was brilliant. He looked out over the edge and barely spied the mosaic raindrops on the ground below. That would be the last thing he ever saw. A gun fired. He was dead. The murderer took the formula from his pocket, pushed him over the edge and was gone. The rain fell, washing away the blood.

The doctor arrived; she cried for the strange man's death. And the sky cried with her.

Paul Hughes *is a contributing editor for CNET, a blogger for Amazon and alt-weekly* The Stranger, *a copy writer for game companies such as Wizards of the Coast and Xbox, and one of the authors behind the* BEASTS! *series from Fantagraphics. Paul also led the team that created the Greenwood Space Travel Supply Co., the "front" for 826 Seattle. When it rains, you can find him sitting by an open window, reading a magazine from cover to cover.*

THE UNKNOWABLE ROYAL

by Paul Hughes

SHELBY, MONTANA had one street and twelve saloons. The city leaders met in the back room of one of those saloons — the Red Dog — in midsummer of 1923 and formed a plan to "put little ol' Shelby on the map," in the words of Mayor Jim Johnson. They bid what was an incredible sum at the time — $250,000 — to host a world-championship prizefight on July 4, between Jack Demspey and Tommy Gibbons. Royal Brougham, a young sportswriter for Seattle's first newspaper, the *Post-Intelligencer*, went to cover the fight and learn how Shelby would achieve its "fistic dream," "even if it has to plaster a mortgage on the town hall to pay the bill," according to Brougham's front-page story. Shelby was "whooping 'er up," with fans "pouring in via Pullman, auto, pony, airplane, and brake beam."

"The stage was set for the most incredible, inconceivable, weird, and whacky prize fight promotion in the long history of the cauliflower-ear pastime," Brougham wrote in a later story. "Overnight the community of 2,000 inhabitants mushroomed into a seething mob of drifters, hoods, gamblers, pickpockets, and their paramours.... There was a bulge on every hip, either a gun or a pint."

"The crowd banked around the ring had to be the most incredible, heterogeneous collection of oddballs in prize fight history," wrote Brougham. "Massed in ringside seats on one side was a score of Blackfeet Indians, resplendent in full war regalia. Cattle barons in wide Stetsons, cow and sheep hands in Levis, New York dudes in Abercrombie and Fitch cowboy suits, well-known mobsters from Chicago and painted ladies in all their finery.... A part of the scene was Wild Bill Lyons, Dempsey's bodyguard, sporting leather chaps, a six-shooter on each hip." The Blackfeet had purportedly inducted the popular challenger, Gibbons, into their tribe as "Chief Thunderbird." After the fight, Dempsey said to Brougham, "Some of those Injuns had long hunting knives and tomahawks. You notice I did most of my fighting on the other side of the ring."

Royal Brougham Way runs east to west, separating Seattle's two stadiums: Qwest Field, home of the Seahawks and Sounders, and Safeco Field, home of the Mariners. Before the Kingdome was demolished in 2000 to make room for Qwest Field, the street used to run along the south side of the Kingdome—a building that Royal Brougham lobbied vociferously to have built, and in which he suffered a fatal heart attack in 1978, in the final minutes of a Broncos-Seahawks game.

It's safe to say that every sports fan in Seattle has walked across Royal Brougham Way at some point, even if it's hard to find anyone who knows who Royal Brougham was. And despite the existence of tens of thousands of stories written by him—and many stories written by Brougham's colleagues about him—questions about who he truly was remain.

Brougham dropped out of Franklin High School and joined the *P-I* as a copy boy in 1910, at age sixteen—a "peppy little fellow in short pants," according to the "Interesting Personalities" section of the *Seattle Daily Journal of Commerce*, which profiled Brougham after he became "the nation's youngest managing editor of a large metropolitan daily" in 1925.

It was around this time that Brougham was present for what can only be described as the invention of liveblogging: "Our circulation manager megaphoned the inning-by-inning progress of the World Series to thousands of fans who jammed the street in front of the Union Street Office. I was the breathless runner who carried the play-by-play results from the wire to the announcer."

A YOUNG ROYAL.

Brougham worked for the *P-I* for nearly seven decades, writing something like eighteen thousand columns, well over ten million words. He was called both the "dean of American sportswriters" and—ten days before his death at eighty-four—the "King Tut of American journalism."

By the time Brougham died in 1978, the letters on his typewriter—which he called his "little old mill"—had been completely worn off, according to colleague Emmett Watson (another Seattle institution). The space bar was worn down to the metal in one spot, where Watson said that Brougham "nervously tapped with his fist as he strained for just the right phrase, the right punch-line, to quicken the beat of a story." It's unclear if Watson was describing Brougham's first typewriter, or one of many.

Stories by colleagues described Brougham as simultaneously self-effacing and a self-promoter, a combination of P. T. Barnum and Forrest Gump, a man who had brushes—by chance or by his own maneuvering—with world-famous figures like Will Rogers, Charlie Chaplin, FDR, even Hitler (while covering the 1936 Olympics). Two of his closest lifelong friends were Jack Dempsey and Babe Ruth. One anecdote puts Brougham and Babe Ruth on the roof of the *P-I* building, with the Bambino autographing balls and throwing them down to a crowd of cheering kids. Billy Graham introduced Brougham as "Mr. Seattle" at a Crusade in the Kingdome in 1976, the largest event ever held there. At the time, Brougham was supposed to be recovering at Swedish Medical Center from a fall (Graham had visited him there twice, where Brougham had left a note on his pillow saying, "Wake me up—I can sleep anytime"), but Brougham convinced his son-in-law Dewey Soriano (former owner of the short-lived Seattle Pilots) to smuggle him out of Swedish in a wheelchair.

Brougham crossed his boss, the publishing giant William Randolph Hearst, by refusing to run fluff pieces about movie star Marion Davies because he disapproved of her affair with the married Hearst. He still managed to get invited to dinners at Hearst Castle, alongside

Davies, Carole Lombard, and William Powell. He called it "a namedropper's dream."

Royal Brougham was the Platonic ideal of the American newspaperman—the kind of guy you'd see in a movie, rushing into a wooden phone booth to file a story, dictating from some scrawled notes in a single take. He's the sort of character that doesn't exist anymore, or doesn't seem to, in an industry that itself is rapidly disappearing.

Accounts of his life are tantalizing and brief, and often conflicting. Another recollection from Watson observed: "He likes to play this folksy, grandpa role of the ultimate innocent, but underneath is a native, professional shrewdness that would dazzle a pawnbroker." And Watson made Brougham's *P-I* sound not so different from the scene in Shelby, Montana: "The office he reigned over for so many years was an incredible mixture: half-illiterate copy boys, drunks, down-and-out fighters, pastors, priests, politicians, athletes, gamblers, pimps, you name it. And an endless procession of students he helped through school."

The students represent another theme in Brougham's life, his devout faith and recurring role as a Good Samaritan. He was a Baptist, and he taught Sunday School for over forty years. When his sports department faced pay cuts in the Depression, he surreptitiously arranged to have all the cuts taken out of his own salary. And after the man who hired him, Portus Baxter, retired in 1920, Brougham finagled a way to keep Baxter on retainer for $5 a week. Brougham ran his errands and even cut Baxter's hair for him for decades. When Baxter died in 1962, he left Brougham a large estate, described in varying accounts as "nearly $300,000" or "$400,000 in blue-chip stocks." Brougham said he wasn't aware of Baxter's fortune. ("Whoever heard of a sportswriter who could add up to that much anyway?")

Four years later, Brougham used $250,000 of the inheritance to set up a foundation for "needy young people... to continue their education in church-related schools and colleges." ("I'm just giving the money spent to enrich back to where it came from. I don't see anything startling about it.... Besides it will be an interesting change to be sort of poor again. And it will keep a guy humble.") The story received wide coverage at the time, including an article in *Time* magazine, which noted that Brougham also gave $150,000 to his married daughter, Alice Soriano. Emmet Watson, upon hearing Brougham's decision to set up the foundation, reportedly said, "You are a freak."

But all these stories about Royal Brougham are just that: stories, old ones now, often told and retold by colleagues who—by the habits of their trade—reflexively burnished details into the most compact and memorable fragments. Brougham's own writing was rarely revealing in any personal way. Brougham was a sportswriter, hailing from the branch of journalism perhaps most obsessed with manufacturing narrative, and in his folksy, prosaic columns— which often ended with scattered collections of fractured notes, his trademark "Chitter Chatter"—he seemed to be just another character, often referring to himself as "Your Old Neighbor."

Brougham attended a gala in his honor at the Washington Athletic Club ten days before he died, at which the mayor and county executive formally decreed October 20th "Royal

Brougham Appreciation Day." The event opened with several telegrams praising his accomplishments. What only a few fellow staffers knew, according to a story written by *P-I* sportswriter Dan Fraley after Brougham's death, was that Brougham himself had written the telegrams—a newsroom prank, consistent with a life of self-invention.

The old man's swagger that night was classic Brougham. He paraphrased what he thought legendary fight promoter Jack Hurley might say: "I've been on some pretty good swindles in my time, but I've never seen this many people pay this much money to see a bow-legged sportswriter sitting at a head table in a rented tuxedo." Given the number of black-tie dinners Brougham attended in his life, he surely should have, and could have, bought a tuxedo—and maybe he did—but he got a lot of mileage out of that joke. At the same event, he also said, "I'd tell you some more stories except my eyesight is fading in this two-bit light they've given me up here. And besides, I've gotta get this monkey suit back to Bonney-Watson." Bonney-Watson is a mortuary.

Brougham was also a constant fund-raiser and civic booster, and the list of board memberships and honors he received is almost ridiculously long. A description by one colleague represents a common sentiment: "In a lot of ways, Brougham was one of the most powerful men in the state. Not just in sports. In any field. When he crooked a finger at them, they came."

Near the end of Husky football's disappointing 1947 season, under coach Ralph "Pest" Welch, Brougham wrote this in a column: "Ralph Welch will be making his last appearance as Washington football coach next Saturday. The big, likeable leader of the Huskies will be replaced after this year, definitely and positively. The former Purdue All-American's doom is sealed, signed and will be delivered at the conclusion of the present season." But according to later *P-I* sportswriter Dan Fraley, "There was no source to this revelation. It was Brougham's wish. The coach was re-moved a month later." Bill Sears, another former *P-I* copy boy and publicist for the Seattle Pilots and Seattle University, elaborat-ed: "He fired a couple of Husky football coaches. He fired them in the paper. Pest Welch was one of them. I don't think Pest ever knew it."

BROUGHAM ANNOUNCING ON
KOMO RADIO.

Emmet Watson also re-members that Brougham "fought long and loud for bigger and bet-ter playfields as 'living memori-als' to the dead of WWII, 'instead of statues of some guy sitting on an iron horse.'" And "long before it became fashionable to give blacks a better break, he was cajoling, ranting, and shaming the citizens of Seattle— into desegregating our lily-white golf courses and bowling alleys. He chided the UW for not recruiting such great local black players as Brennan King and Homer Harris."

Brougham was charming and idiosyncratic, a perfectly designed anecdote engine. Many stories revolve around his being a rigid teetotaler who never swore in a booze-soaked and profanity-intensive profession. Georg Meyers, at the competing *Seattle Times*, remembers covering the UW rowing crew alongside Brougham in Moscow, when Brougham even turned down a farewell vodka toast from their interpreter: "'Royal, this young man is trying to be hospitable,' I said. 'You may damage international relations—or worse, hurt his feelings—if you refuse to join the toast. We will never tell anyone. No one will ever know.' 'I will know,' Brougham said, as he turned down his empty glass."

Paradoxically, he earned a reputation for attracting drunks—like one constant comic foil for him, "Cowboy" Joe Ryan, the mayor of Bothell. Ryan's lesser feats included painting all the fire hydrants in town white, "so dogs could see them at night." Brougham remembered that the Seattle City Council lodged only a "mild protest" when Ryan rode his horse Silver into Seattle's Olympic Hotel while singing his theme song ("Ryan Rides Again") and asking for twin beds, yelling, "Send up to my room a club sandwich and a bale of hay!" before the police arrived. Ryan and Brougham clearly both enjoyed the attention that came from their mock feud, with episodes such as the time Ryan led "a full brass band playing Irish airs" in front of Brougham's house at midnight on St. Patrick's Day, waving a green-ribboned shillelagh as a baton.

The stories about Brougham are full of questions and gaps. For example, it's difficult to learn anything about Alice, his wife of fifty years, who was an invalid for the last two decades of her life, after a stroke paralyzed half of her body. Brougham trafficked in embellishment, and now he's lost to it—a man who was so well-known at one time that when somebody robbed his house in Magnolia then tried to use one of his credit cards at a store downtown, the clerk said, "You're not Royal Brougham, not even close." Or so the story goes.

Emmett Watson wrote about a sort of sportswriter tontine from the fight at Shelby. Some of the biggest names in journalism at the time were there — Westbrook Pegler, Bill Corum, Damon Runyon, Ring Lardner, and Hype Igoe. The young Brougham wasn't very accomplished at that point, but the other writers liked him, and he was later invited into a "last man club" of Shelby sportswriters — in which they all chipped in on a case of champagne, which would go to the last surviving member of the club. Pegler was a "tough, mean, opinionated columnist" in Watson's estimation (a charitable assessment of the fire-breathing conservative, the first columnist to ever win a Pulitzer). When Pegler visited Seattle in the '60s, Watson called him to ask about the "last man club": "Since I knew, as a spiritual certainty, that Royal Brougham is practically immortal, I was shocked. Not only was he no worse than 2-5 to out-live them all, he had never taken a drink in his life. 'Mr. Pegler,' I said, 'Royal Brougham doesn't drink.' 'Maybe he doesn't now,' said Pegler, 'but he did then. Right along with the rest of us.'"

This didn't fit the Royal Brougham narrative — and Watson, apparently, didn't buy it; "He was no man to stand corrected, but I had to say it. 'Mr. Pegler, you are wrong. Royal has never had a drink in his life.' There was a long hostile silence on the line. 'Okay,' Pegler said finally, 'maybe you're right.'"

But Watson didn't let it end there. He approached Brougham, "struck by a mischievous, even fiendish impulse…. 'I have been talking to Pegler,' I told Brougham. 'He says you used to booze it up at Shelby.' R. B. twitched with alarm. He knew that Pegler could get enraged by anyone who challenged his veracity. 'Furthermore,' I went on, lying cruelly, 'Pegler says he's going to write a column about Shelby. He will mention how you boozed it up.' There was a soft, audible sigh. 'Oh, no...' he groaned."

Brougham died at a turning point in Seattle sports. He spent much of his career preoccupied with hockey, rowing, boxing, hydroplane racing, and Pacific Coast League baseball (the Seattle Rainiers were the local team, originally named the Indians, but renamed after they were bought by Rainier Brewery, which was named after the mountain). When he had his heart attack at the Kingdome, the Seahawks were only in their third season. The Mariners had just finished their second. The SuperSonics made it to the finals a few months before Brougham died and lost, to the Washington Bullets. They would go to the finals again the next year and defeat the Bullets—giving Seattle its first professional sports championship since the Metropolitans won the Stanley Cup in 1917, defeating the Montreal Canadiens. Brougham, of course, covered that series in great detail—just as he did the Met's next shot at the title two years later, when the finals were canceled after just five games because of the flu epidemic. Brougham wrote of the throngs of spectators wearing cotton masks and players from both teams dropping to the ice from exhaustion and fever.

Eddie O'Brien, a former Pittsburgh Pirates infielder and Seattle University athletic director, was interviewed by the *P-I*'s Dan Raley after Brougham's death. "Don't think anybody really knew him," said O'Brien. "His columns were gossip, and I think that's what people missed. A great deal were inaccurate, but everybody used to rush to see what he had in there."

Eighteen-year-old **Autumn Straker** *lives, for now, in the Greenwood neighborhood, in a home with five televisions but no couch. She's afraid of swimming in open water, but not of cutting her own hair. When it rains, she likes to read the old saved text messages on her phone, or pines for Discovery Park.*

UP IN SMOKE

by Autumn Straker

IT WAS TUESDAY, the most useless day of the whole week. It wasn't warm enough for just short sleeves yet, though the magnolia blooms had begun to peel apart so it was just about warm enough for some people to say it was spring. A woman stood against the wall near the Cross Walk Bar entrance and smoked her Lucky cigarette—a bit too Freudian for the daytime. Standing there, watching the smoke exhaust into the sky, she wondered what she was doing.

"Has it always been like this?"

She just wanted a man so badly; a man to call her own. A man to call her…

Hanging out in midday bars to be where the mat-swept men sat, usually alone and with plenty of time to murder, her plan to fall in love here seemed foolproof.

She always imagined that finding love in a bar was something dangerous, like mythology, or high school. All-or-nothing dangerous. The idea of this loomed and consumed her like a long shadow. A little more anxious than shade, and available for a little less time. But, like all original sinister plans, the idea came to her like clumsy rummaging hands under blankets. And because she woke up too early to dream and went to bed too late to sleep, it didn't seem half wrong to her to think that the same men that looked for women in the evening would be waiting in layaway during the day.

She was a fairly good-looking woman as far as older women go, but it was hard to ignore that she looked somehow insincere. Her face was like a Hallmark card, and her smile had that same meaningless cuteness, like figuring out that "dog" and "god" used the same letters or that Toyota was almost the same forwards and backwards.

Her whole look, with her flat black hair like background velvet in a diamond bracelet ad, was reminiscent of noir but without any of the romance or suspense of the genre.

But she smoked enough to have that count towards her look, which was another major reason why her plan was so transparent. She didn't even drink; she smoked.

She chain-smoked. Not chain-smoked in the sense that she smoked one after another after another, lighting up the tips from the butts (even though she did do that), or even in some sort of metaphorical sense of a way of saying that her addictive smoking habit was like being chained up. In her most syncopated smoke break, her chain-smoking was like a chain necklace: an expensive luxury for her to show off. To be seen. Though, it would be more accurate to say "seem" instead of "seen," because, while they both mean "appear," the difference between the words and what she wanted to accomplish was something too delicate for her chiseled look.

But by the way she looked, she seemed like the kind

of woman who didn't wash her makeup off before she went to bed because when she was a kid there was a retirement home across the street and one night an old man feel asleep with a lit cigarette in the ashtray next to his bed and during the night he flung the blankets over and caught them on fire. Then the firemen came and the ambulances came and they put the fire out and pulled the old burnt man out of his sheets and put a mask over his face and put him through the back ambulance doors. And she and her family and everybody on the block came out to watch.

And because of this, she always fantasized about looking nice in case that ever happened to her: in case firemen would have to pull her from her bed in her singed nightgown with their uniformed arms and hand her to the EMTs who would perform mouth-to-mouth resuscitation and when she woke up would propose to her because she was most beautiful woman they had ever saved from an apartment fire.

Really, though, the old burnt man died in the ambulance on the way to the hospital, and she never even had the chance to fall asleep with a cigarette lit because she couldn't even smoke in the apartment complex she lived in and the smoke detectors went off when she made toast. But still, that morning, after a silent night without firemen at her window, when she heard on the news that the Greenwood Arsonist had struck again, she couldn't help feeling she missed out as she took a shower and her mascara dropped down her face like dog pee down a pile of summer-dried cinder blocks.

And all this with her had been going on for a long time, but these things weren't what she was wondering about. Sitting around through the midday hours in bars, she was really wondering about the men and if they had they always been so mad and so cold.

It used to be, like the inevitability of a mosquito bite in August, men would talk to her. Their words just as annoying and their hands just as itchy. But now it was different. Their hearts, like the open, begging hands of children, had turned into the palms of veterans at the off-ramp of Highway 99. Now, during the day the men didn't want even one little piece of her because they came to bars to forget and be old men and because any woman must have been worse off than them to be hanging out in a place like that.

So when they see this woman show up, looking all right with her tan and smoky eyes, in the last place they would expect, it wasn't that they were too foolish for women or not clever enough to talk. It was just that they were too used to there being a difference between reality and fantasy. Like the difference between the way a woman's thighs look in your headlights and the way they look in your passenger seat: when something's far enough away to wish on, your thoughts turn extravagant, but when it's close enough to what you've dreamed about, you freeze.

Turning away in a wasted wind, she almost made a connection.

"Did it only begin to be this way since I moved up here from L.A.?"

Zoë Newton *is ten, and one of her favorite places in Seattle is a place she calls "the dangerous playground" because it has lots of things that spin you around and make you dizzy. She probably wouldn't go there when it's raining. She might be hanging out with her dad, though. She admires him because he helps her out and they both like to draw and read. "Reading is just what I do," she says. "It pretty much just makes me feel better about anything."*

THE OUTCASTS

by Zoë Newton

TORI, MICK, AND CORY ran back to the Space Needle with loaves of challah bread and pepper jack cheese from Cinnamon Works in hand. The trio had lost the old man with the cane. Cory took a hungry bite of bread.

"That was a close one," he breathed.

"It would have been easier if you didn't knock over the bananas," Tori shot back.

"Maybe you shouldn't have tried to pick them up!" Cory yelled at her.

"STOP FIGHTING!" Mick shouted.

Tori crossed her arms but said nothing. Being out until the Space Needle closed every day was hard. They would always pretend they were unaccompanied minors on a tour vacation. They would just try to memorize the histories of all of Seattle's famous landmarks.

Mick picked the lock and they went inside. Every time Tori was in there, it made her dizzy. There was Space Needle merchandise EVERYWHERE. The kids rested their heads on Space Needle pillows and pulled Space Needle blankets over themselves.

Tori had run away from her home in Tacoma after her mother remarried. Cory was from Forks and had hated his little sister. Mick was a mystery.

They all went to sleep so they could get up before nine o'clock when the Space Needle opened!

Pip walked casually down the street at the Pike Place Market, trying not to be caught with the money she had pick-pocketed from the tall, black-haired lady. Looking behind her, she crashed into three dirty kids. The one on the left had long amber hair and sharp hazel eyes. The one in the middle had short blond hair with blue eyes. The one on the right was tall with red hair piled on his head.

"Er... hello," said the girl on the left. "Where are your parents?"

"Orphan," Pip said. "Hated my foster dad. Ran away. I'm Pip."

"Tori," said Tori. "This is Cory and Mick. We all ran away from home. At least, I think all of us did." She added, giving Mick a sideways glance.

"Charmed," said Mick, ignoring what Tori said and quickly swiping an apple from the stand next to them. "Hey you!" said a gruff voice behind them. They all turned their heads. An angry-looking man swung his arm toward Mick's head, but Mick dodged just in time.

"RUN!" Cory screamed. They ran to the Seattle Center once they were away from the market.

"Where do you live?" Cory asked Pip.

"Er… nowhere," Pip said.

"Come with us," said Mick, biting into the apple.

"Really?" said Pip.

"'Course," said Tori. "We can all get something good from running away."

"Really? I've never told you where I came from?" Mick said to Tori, Cory, and Pip. "Really? Never? You can't be serious. Fine. I was abandoned at the doorstep of a woman named Lorelei Finnigan."

"Lorelei Finnigan?" Pip asked. "I stole her wallet!"

Everybody then turned their stares to Pip, who held up a brown leather wallet. Tori and Cory then looked back at Mick, who gaped at Pip as if she had just said the world was about to explode. "But… I ran away because she… died," Mick squeaked.

Pip opened the wallet and pulled out the driver's license. "Well, it is Lorelei Finnigan." Pip looked uncomfortable. "Oh… this is awkward." Cory gave a slight laugh at Pip.

"Maybe we can track her down!" Mick said hopefully. Everybody looked uneasy, "OK…" said Tori, "I guess it's for the best."

"Great. How much money's in there, Pip?" Mick asked.

"Forty bucks."

"Awesome. We can buy bus tickets. What's the address on the license?"

"257 North Seventy-fourth Street."

"Bus number five has a stop near there," Mick said, triumphantly. "I'll have a home again!"

—

"How do you know about this stuff, Mick?" Cory asked, while he and his three friends ran to a bus stop.

"I look at bus schedules."

They reached the bus stop for the number five. Soon a big green bus drove up to the stop with the word METRO written in yellow letters. When the door opened, several people got off, then the bus driver beckoned for them to come on. The kids slowly stepped on and gave the bus driver three dollars. They all sat down. None of them spoke. Their best friend was about to leave.

Soon the bus pulled up to a busy street where the kids needed to get off. Once the bus drove away Mick shouted "This way!" and the three began to run after him. Tori, Cory, and Pip were all hungry, but Mick seemed so happy that they didn't want to stop him and eat at the Wing Dome. They ran until all of them but Mick were worn out. "You guys can go back. I'll go myself." Mick formed a group hug with his friends. They reluctantly let him go and he ran along the sunny streets.

"I'll miss him," Cory sniffed. Tori sighed. "Me too."

Mick padded up the walkway to house number 257. The house was short and pink with green shutters. He walked up the front steps and rapped on the door. It cracked open and a tall woman with grey hair peeked out. She took one look at Mick and her eyes widened greatly. She opened the door completely and whispered, "Mick?"

"Lory?" Mick replied. "I thought you were dead."

Lorelei hesitated. "I have a horrible confession to make," she said. "I faked my death because I didn't want a son." Mick frowned and began to turn to walk away.

"But *now I do*!" Mick turned around, smiled, and hugged her. "We have to celebrate! What food do you like? What music should be played? What—"

"Wait." Mick interrupted. "There's something I want to do first…"

"What's that paper on the floor?" asked Pip, pointing at the blue paper on the floor.

"I don't know…" Tori said. She walked up to it and picked it up. Written in tiny dark blue were the words:

To Tori, Cory, and Pip

"It's for us!" said Cory excitedly. "Unfold it!" Tori unfolded the paper and began to read aloud:

Dear friends,

How are you? I hope you're well. I miss you and I am very sorry I left you. I told Lorelei about you and she would like to adopt the three of you as well. We will come to pick you up tomorrow at 8:00 a.m. sharp.

Sincerely, Mick

"It's from Mick!" Tori announced. "We're going to have a home again!"

Everybody whooped and became jittery. They could barely sleep though they needed it. They had a wonderful day ahead of them.

Isabel Canning *returned to writing after her career as a rock and roll sensation ended.*

DEUS EX MACHINA

FROM *When a Sentence Ends in a Surprising Gazebo*

by Isabel Canning

I HEAR THE scratching of trees against trees, a hollowed-out branch locked in never-ending war with chalk-white fibers covered in slivers of blue and red.

I see the darkness creeping into the pulsating red organ that resides in a hollow cage with walls of flesh and bars of bone.

I know the secrets whispered in a hollow tube that forever siphons sound to the lump of neurons that looks and smells like blue cheese but controls our every move.

I am a machine programmed to think and act uniquely toward other machines, all controlled by the quivering organ lodged in our heads, which is kept alive, in turn, by the organ in the chest of bones, muscles, and skin.

I am a human being.

I feel the hardened gray rock beneath my feet as I take in the green and brown colors around me, with round orbs that were implanted in my skull at the beginning of my sorry existence.

I am encased within a globe of green and blue that I walk upon endlessly, never stopping for a moment.

I see tiny machines with simpler minds and different attributes than mine, such as appendages for flight and a clear, melodious call to others of their kind.

I know the way to a large, green box by heart, furnished with necessities such as food and drink.

I am greeted by two machines. The smaller one shrieks delightedly and embraces the appendages I use for walking.

I live on planet Earth.

The larger machine opens her speaking tube and asks me how the interaction area was, and whether I cranked my speed dial to run.

I find a plate with cut-up meat tubes and tomato paste, and a glass of clear liquid nearby.

I dip the meat into the paste and shovel it into my speaking tube, where it is mashed and sent to the part of my body used for digesting.

I go over to a cushion and use my ocular organs to scan a rectangular object filled with two-dimensional thoughts and ideas.

I live with my mother and sister.

I am on a large cushion covered by smaller cushions. I shut my ocular organs and let the quivering lump in my head take over.

All is quiet in my sleeping compartment. The only sound that remains is the steady beat of the pulsating red organ that resides in the hollow cage with walls of flesh and bars of bone.

I am a human being.

Charles R. Cross *is a Seattle writer and the author of seven books, including biographies of Jimi Hendrix, Kurt Cobain and Bruce Springsteen. He was also the longtime editor of the Seattle entertainment magazine* The Rocket. *A Northwest native, he will never be seen with an umbrella, but thinks waterproof books would be a good invention for Northwest readers.*

ELVIS IN SEATTLE, 1962

FROM *Seattle Magazine, 1992*

by Charles R. Cross

ON SEPTEMBER 17, 1962, Elvis Presley awoke from a deep slumber, looked out the window of his 14th floor suite in the New Washington Hotel, and saw a city that would be shocked by the news that day that he wore no underwear.

Elvis was in Seattle to film "It Happened at the World's Fair," and anything about Elvis, even his underwear, or lack thereof, was front-page news. This was an era in Seattle when if you hosted a cocktail party for your neighbors, it might end up in the society pages of the papers. And if you were the biggest star in the world, and you went commando, it was bound to get people talking.

The summer of 1962 in the Northwest was a season filled with optimism, benevolence, and cultural awakening. With the King, the World's Fair, the Monorail, and the Space Needle, Seattle got its first national attention. The Space Needle was on the cover of *Life* magazine twice that year, and on the cover of *Sunset*, and many other publications. It was as if the summer of 1962 was one big debutante ball for the coming out of what was then called the Queen City (only later was the Emerald City used as a nickname for Seattle).

And, like many debutantes, Seattle glowed in the spotlight, particularly with the attention thrown on the Fair, which was officially titled the "Century 21 Exposition." The theme of the Exposition was "the future," and that future seemed unlimited at the time. Build a flying saucer on a pole? Great idea: and soon the Space Needle was looming over the rest of the city. In a fraction of the time Seattle spent arguing over whether to build a waterfront tunnel to replace the Alaskan Way Viaduct, the city approved the idea of the Needle, and saw it constructed in less than a year. Before it was finished, the iconic design was adorning t-shirts, ashtrays, and saltshakers. And that same year, the Monorail was also built to carry the expected tourists from downtown to the Fair. It was a time in Seattle when anything seemed possible, and when civic leaders dreamed big, and with a decidedly science fiction flair.

The building boom paid off. More than ten million people attended the 1962 World's Fair, including Richard Nixon, Igor Stravinsky, and Ray Bradbury. It was one of the few fairs of that era to actually make a profit, probably because it was also the first to showcase a Thai restaurant. "The long term effect of the Fair on Seattle was enormous," says Jay Rockey, a publicist for the event, who later started his own P.R. firm. "As far as national and international attention, nothing else has ever done for Seattle what the World's Fair did in 1962…. People believed in it, and furthermore, they believed in themselves."

In many ways, the 1962 World's Fair was the beginning of modern Seattle.

In 1962, Seattle was still a sleepy port city, best known as the headquarters for the Boeing Company, which built the planes that won World War II. In that era, long before Microsoft or Starbucks, Seattle was a blue-collar port town that made boats and planes. A three-bedroom house near Greenlake cost $12,500 in 1962, and a pair of white slacks at the Fredrick and Nelson department store would set you back five dollars. In the era before software and dot com millionaires, one of the exhibits at the World's Fair predicted executives would eventually make as much as "$12,000 a year."

Before the Fair, Seattle greatest contribution to the national culture was the word "Skid Row," invented to describe how logs were slid down Yesler Way to a pier. But the Fair changed how others perceived Seattle, and how Seattle perceived itself. "You can attribute a lot of Seattle's cultural changes to the World's Fair," says Cyrus Noe, who did P.R. for the event. "The Seattle Rep came out of the Fair, as did the beginning of our healthy theater scene." Noe reminds us that before the World's Fair, a local right-wing columnist named Westbook Pigler once called Seattle "a Methodist camp meeting town."

If the 1962 Seattle World's Fair suggested the future, it also showcased some of Seattle's sordid past, which was anything other than a church camp. One of most popular attractions at the Fair was a strip show run by the infamous Gracie Hansen, and an adults-only puppet show designed by Sid and Marty Krofft. It was as if Seattle could show off modern ambitions, but not yet break from the town's original history of bars and brothels. Though Hansen's "Paradise

International" revue was not that different from many of the bawdy palaces that lined First Avenue in that day, some questioned if a strip show should be part of the Fair. "People were aghast," remembers Dennis Flannigan, a Washington State legislator. "Still, they loved it. It was as pasteurized as sex was at the time, but it was big news. Gracie Hansen took the state by storm. Within a month, she owned the town.". Before the Fair, says Flannigan, "Seattle was just Tacoma large." After the Fair, Seattle was a world-class city, and it never looked back.

Hansen's strip show was one of the most talked-about aspects of the Seattle World's Fair, but it actually drew smaller crowds than the science exhibits. The "Office of Tomorrow," complete with the rotary dial direct telephones, was a perennial crowd pleaser, as was a futuristic house with automated appliances. "I remember going to the 'House of the Future,' and thinking that all we'd do in the future is wait in lines all day," says John Keister, of the television show *Almost Live.* "This vision of the future was that everything would be so automated we'd never have to lift a muscle for anything. It was completely ridiculous, and I loved it."

Some of the futuristic exhibits from 1962 turned out to be surprising prescient. General Electric advertised their televisions as children's "invisible playmate," which would one day be able to play "games." The IBM exhibit said that the future was in computers, but they also hedged their bets by showcasing their innovative "Selectric Typewriter." Another exhibit showed "the office worker of tomorrow," who would toil for "twenty-four hour days" the display predicted. It was the perfect time to have a fair about the future because it was a time when Seattle believed anything was possible. "There was even an exhibit I remember on Communism," says Keister, "and what a horrible life that was. I was really moved by it, and scared. There'd be these little kids there crying to their parents, saying, 'Mommy, don't make me be a Communist!'"

And if that exhibit wasn't enough to terrify the kiddies of Seattle, there was a real, live Communist even. Cyrus Noe ended up with the job of escorting around Russian General Gherman Titov, who had beaten John Glenn into space, and also wanted to beat him to the Mongolian Beef Grill at the Fair. Glenn visited as well, on a different day, and in his honor the Monorail was temporarily renamed "Friendship Seven." A bevy of politicians made much-publicized trips to Seattle for the Fair, including Lyndon Johnson, Dwight Eisenhower, and many more. Iranian students cheered when the Shah of Iran showed, and huge crowds applauded Britain's Prince Phillip. Cultural legends like Ed Sullivan, Ella Fitzgerald, Issac Stern, Nat King Cole, Van Cliburn, Josh White, and Benny Goodman also came.

Jay Rockey was in charge of publicity for the Fair and he says his job was to get a different headline every day. "They couldn't keep writing the same story about how beautiful the fair was," he says. "We had to get a new dateline every day, so something had to happen." Rockey remembers that when Richard Nixon toured the Fair there weren't headlines, since Nixon was no longer in office, and had pledged that he'd left politics for good. "He came as a private person, not a politician, because he wanted to see the Fair. He was a very pleasant and down-to-earth guy."

If Nixon was an everyman in those days, Elvis Presley was

ELVIS PRESLEY PRESENTING A GIFT TO WASHINGTON GOVERNOR ALBERT ROSELLINI,
AT THE MONORAIL STATION, WESTLAKE AVENUE, SEPTEMBER 5, 1962

his antithesis, a star who couldn't leave his hotel room without getting mobbed. Elvis's every move—everything he ate, or where he shopped—was reported to an adoring public. It was when a wardrobe consultant to "It Happened at the World's Fair" was questioned about Presley's wardrobe that the little nugget dropped that Elvis wore no underwear. But just as interesting, if less reported, was what Elvis did wear. For the film he had ten suits, and each cost $285, a fortune in those days. He had thirty shirts (he sweated a lot) at $10 each; four sport jackets at $200; two cashmere overcoats at $225; fifteen pairs of pants at $85; and fifty-five ties at $7 each.

Fair publicists had to soak any tidbit they could out of the film set, since the actual movie wouldn't premiere until 1963, long after the Fair was over, so Hollywood couldn't help boost attendance. But having Elvis touring the Space Needle wasn't a bad way of attracting teenagers to the Fair.

Rita Baeyen was one such Seattle teenager, who headed down with the dream of meeting Elvis. "I was twelve at the time, and very much in love with Elvis," she recalls. "A girlfriend and I went down to the Fair because we read in the paper that Elvis was going to be there. There were crowds of young girls, and Elvis was going through them on this slow-moving tram. When he came by us, I stuck out my autograph book, and handed it to him, and he signed it. He gave me this little wink too, which just about knocked me over. I was surprised he'd make eye contact. It wasn't really a seductive wink, but it was more a sign that he knew what I was thinking. I'll always remember that wink."

Elvis Presley died in 1977, but the Space Needle still endures. It remains as probably the most memorable monument Seattle will ever build, for a World's Fair or for anything else. "I knew the Fair was going to be something the moment they decided to build the Space Needle," Jay Rockey says. "As that thing was built, it looked just like a United Way thermometer showing how much interest there was in the Fair: As the Needle became taller, the interest in the World's Fair got greater. It still looks great to me. Not only did they build the thing in record time, but the blooming thing looks timeless. It might be even more appropriate today than it was in 1962."

The now deceased Seattle restaurant owner Ivar Haglund was rarely one to talk positively about any restaurant location he didn't own. Yet even to Ivar, the Space Needle looked great. "The farther away you get, the better it looks," he said.

FORECAST: Downpour

Bharti Kirchner *has written four novels, four cookbooks, and hundreds of articles, short stories, and essays. Kirchner says she lives a multi-faceted life going to art shows, movies, lectures, and traveling, all of which informs her writing. When it rains, she likes to get lost reading something intriguing and possibly historical. Kirchner has been a Seattle resident for twenty-five years and finds nothing more comforting than the aroma of baking a fruit tart on a drizzly day.*

AH, BAKLAVA

by Bharti Kirchner

THE FIRST FEW icy drops of a sudden squall tattooed my back, watery little needles that heralded another gloomy Seattle morning. A chilly wind from nearby Puget Sound gusted at the speed of a train, kicking up short choppy waves. A sea smell pervaded the air. As though in an epiphany, a streak of lightning etched itself across the sky. My shopping expedition to Pike Place Market thus interrupted, I dashed to the nearest store, the now-defunct Mr. D's Greek Delicacies.

Once inside, in the perfect 68-degree temperature, I savored a heady mélange of aromas—honey, nuts, and other good things. My eyes were drawn to a tray of baklava cut into two-inch wide, diamond-shaped pieces sitting on the counter. Outside the rain showed no sign of subsiding, so I decided to sample a flaky golden slice to pass the time. The first bite nearly overwhelmed my palate. Made of paper-thin sheets of phyllo dough ("leaf" in Greek), Mr. D's pastry was filled with crushed nuts and it oozed with fragrant sugar syrup: a luscious dense torte, if you will.

"It's definitely a change of pace," said a friend, who shared the treat with me.

It was much more than that, this soft, crunchy, sweet sensation, warm from the oven. It brightened my mood and delighted my senses, giving rise to images in my mind of a sunny land, a sultan's palace, and the legendary spice route. Baklava has traveled a long distance to come to Seattle, I concluded.

I had sampled baklava before, in Chicago, San Francisco, and, of course, Greece. But this piece was different. Its fragrance reminded me of roaming through lavender fields. Instead of the traditional walnut filling, it contained hazelnuts. And, as a bonus, I found a dollop of cream tucked away inside, a variation I discovered later to be popular in Iraq.

It was the nineties. Such innovations weren't unknown in our increasingly diverse, food-crazed city even then. You could experiment. You could think big. You could erase boundaries. I envisioned myself combing the neighborhoods, trying different incarnations of baklava, and gathering tips from home cooks and chefs. Thus fired up, I also imagined myself donning an apron and whipping up a big tray of this dessert in the warmth of my kitchen, creating my own little heaven on rain-soaked earth.

"But why the sudden interest in baklava?" another friend asked me. "Isn't it super rich? Cloyingly sweet? Fattening?"

OK, OK. So baklava wasn't exactly an avatar of lean cuisine—I was forced to admit. But I insisted that for all its extravagance, this delicacy still had a few things going for it. It contained no eggs, which many consider a plus. You could replace a portion of its saturated fat with vegetable oil and, without sacrificing the flavor, cut down on the amount of sugar or honey. Also, you needed only a thin slice to satisfy your taste buds.

This last point, however, was open to debate.

No one knows for sure where this confection originated. It was most likely an eastern Mediterranean country or the Middle East. Regardless, many nationalities claim baklava as their own. "Ours is the best," they invariably say in a tone they might use to boast about their education or health care systems.

Although the basic technique doesn't change from country to country, a cook's birthplace definitely determines his or her style of making and serving baklava. That much became clear when I spoke with a Greek-American grandmother. In the old country, she informed me, no holiday would be complete without a slice of this pastry accompanied by cognac, ouzo (a clear, anise-flavored aperitif, practically the national liqueur), or strong Greek coffee. There it was served at home on birthdays, family get-togethers, and any time a friend dropped by for a visit.

Baklava has occasionally been put to other, more unconventional uses as well. "Once I made a large tray of baklava for a grandchild's birthday party and set it out in the yard to cool," the grandmother said. "I was only away for a few minutes but, when I returned, I found that the kids were pelting each other with baklava slices. All those hours of work vanished before my eyes."

I sighed along with her, imagining the treats smashed, wasted, and lying forlornly on the ground, a feast for the ants.

The grandmother then shared a few traditional tips with me, such as flavoring the walnut filling with ground cinnamon and cloves, and using honey, preferably imported from Greece, as the syrup base. She called hers the "most authentic" version.

Eyes twinkling, she added, "But don't ever leave it unattended."

Next, I approached a Lebanese cook. "Surely ours is more refined than the Greeks'," she said. It has a subtle flowery scent that comes from an infusion of either rose water or orange blossom water in the syrup, she explained. Crushed green pistachios are sprinkled on top, making it more colorful and inviting. Ground almonds are blended with the usual walnuts in the filling, resulting in a more complex flavor. "It's also less wet and sticky," she added, meaning that sugar syrup was used sparingly.

Iranians, it turned out, also make baklava. "It was served at my wedding," an Iranian-American woman told me. "Now my wedding anniversaries aren't complete without it." Her festive version incorporates cardamom as part of the filling and saffron, an expensive spice, as an addition to the syrup.

In a mood for more stories, I spoke with George Lagos, an expatriate from Greece and owner of Continental Restaurant and Pastry Shop, an establishment in the University District. Lagos had been supplying Seattleites with this treat for decades. Oddly enough, he said that his baklava had a Filipino accent. His Filipino pastry chef, Rogelio Posadas, had been producing large trays of it, as many as 120 slices per day, for the past 15 years.

Lagos served a delectable slice gratis with my dinner order. Although I didn't detect any unusual ingredients, or anything identifiably Filipino, I wondered about the secrets of this pastry chef. Perhaps observing my wistful look, a fellow diner from the next table, who claimed to be a regular at the restaurant, offered me an insight.

"From what I understand," he said, "it's the cook's state of mind that makes this dessert special."

He sounded philosophical in a way baklava can make you. "What do you mean?" I asked.

"I mean attention to details. I mean patience. I mean an extra something only the cook can give." With that, he closed his eyes to savor the last bite of his baklava.

He was right. Soon enough, I began preparing my own, a lighter, less sweet version that borrowed from many traditions but was also imbued with a few personal touches. After I clarify the butter to remove the milk solids, I brush the phyllo sheets with the golden liquid and place them in a baking pan, alternating each sheet with a layer of crushed walnuts, cinnamon, and cardamom. The addition of a few ground macadamia nuts imparts a unique flavor all my own. Then I bake the ensemble in a preheated oven. For the next hour, I find myself deeply inhaling the exotic perfume that fills the kitchen. But I can't linger at this stage. There is still sugar syrup to be prepared. I do so by heating a mixture of sugar, water, honey, and lemon juice. To that I add a bit of maple syrup, another personal preference. Puffy and golden, the baklava finally emerges from the oven, ready to be drizzled with the thick luscious syrup.

However, it's still not done. I must now leave it at room temperature for a day or two to allow the syrup to be absorbed and the flavors to blend. Only then is the treat ready to be sampled. Only then can I fully cope with the rain.

BAKLAVA
makes 24 pieces

HERE ARE SOME TIPS on working with tissue-paper-thin sheets of phyllo dough. Sold in one-pound packages, phyllo is best if it hasn't been frozen, but boxed phyllo, available refrigerated in supermarkets, also works. Because they contain mostly flour and water and very little oil, phyllo sheets can dry out quickly if exposed to air, and become difficult to manipulate. As you separate the sheets, cover the rest of the supply with a damp tea towel to retain their moisture.

INGREDIENTS

Clarified butter:
    3 sticks (¾ pound) unsalted butter, cut into ¼-inch slices
    ½ cup canola oil

Syrup:

    1 ¼ cups sugar

    ¾ cup water

    2 tablespoons honey

    2 tablespoons maple syrup

    1 tablespoon freshly squeezed lemon juice

Pastry:

    1 pound walnuts, ground to a coarse powder in a blender
      or food processor

    2 tablespoons macadamia nuts, ground to a coarse powder

    1 tablespoon ground cinnamon

    2 teaspoons ground cardamom

    1 pound phyllo dough (about 30 sheets)

Garnish:

    2 to 3 tablespoons crushed pistachios

DIRECTIONS

1. Clarify the butter: Place butter in a heavy saucepan over low heat for 10 to 15 minutes. Skim off the foam from the top and discard. Carefully pour the clear liquid into a bowl through layers of cheesecloth so that none of the sediments at the bottom gets through. Add oil and mix.

2. Combine walnuts, macadamia nuts, cinnamon, and cardamom in a bowl. Preheat oven to 350°F.

3. Coat the bottom of a 9 x 13-inch baking pan with 3 tablespoons butter-oil mixture. Layer 6 phyllo sheets over it, brushing each sheet (or every 2 or 3 sheets) with the butter-oil mixture. Sprinkle about ½ cup of the nut mixture evenly over the top. Layer 3 to 4 sheets over the nuts, brush lightly with the butter-oil mixture and sprinkle another ½ cup or so nut mixture on the top surface. Continue until the nut mixture is used up. Cover the top with 5 to 6 phyllo sheets. Press with your palm to remove any air pockets. Score with a sharp knife, first horizontally, then vertically, and then diagonally into diamond shapes, making sure the knife cuts all the way down. Pour the remaining butter-oil mixture evenly over the top. Bake for 45 to 50 minutes or until golden brown. Remove from oven. Turn off oven.

4. Prepare syrup: While baklava is baking, place sugar and water in a pan and bring to a boil. Reduce heat and cook for about 12 to 15 minutes or until the syrup is thick and coats a spoon. Remove from heat. Add honey, maple syrup, and lemon juice. Just before baklava is ready, reheat the syrup just until hot.

5. As soon as baklava comes out of the oven, pour hot syrup all over the top. Return to oven, which should still be hot, for 2 minutes. Remove from oven and let rest at room temperature for at least a day, preferably two. Serve warm (heated briefly in a 350°F oven) or at room temperature, sprinkled with pistachios.

145

Teri Hein *carries many dozens of eggs weekly in her little convertible from Old Tarboo Farm to members of her egg club in Seattle. Besides that, she is the founding executive director of 826 Seattle and the author of the memoir* Atomic Farmgirl. *When it rains, she can be found reading the Sunday* New York Times *or repotting plants in her greenhouse.*

ADOLPH, A LOVE STORY

by Teri Hein

DURING THE DAY, our chickens roam wherever they please on Old Tarboo Farm. We have this little twenty-five-acre paradise over on the Olympic Peninsula, bought on a whim once between jobs when I had a lot of free time to pursue my hobby of looking at real estate. The farm is on the west side of Hood Canal Bridge, as opposed to our city home on the east side of it; the bridge has become a metaphor for my constant desire to connect the continents of my life.

Jim and I bought the farm, found some hippie farmers to grow the tomatoes, and four years later Adolph came in the mail from Iowa as a chick, along with the rest of our flock, a collection of Buff Orpingtons, Barred Rocks, and Golden Laced Wyandottes.

We named all of them, renaming as necessary when their genders revealed themselves. The ducks, Lucky Duck, Unlucky Duck, and Helen, were all girls. The chickens turned out to be four roosters and ten hens, the latter with names like Wilma and Frida and Brownie. We endured weeks of rooster posturing as Adolph, Red 1, Red 2, and Chuck the Chicken vied for leadership of the flock. Actually, Chuck didn't really vie. He was the flock outcast, a giant white Araucana show chicken that Jim ordered from a designer chicken catalog. Tall with feathered ankles, he pranced around the farm, giving out pathetic mini crows as he danced around the edges of the flock. The other chickens disliked Chuck. Even the tiny hens would chase and peck him if he tried to eat in their proximity.

Early on, Red 2 mysteriously disappeared, which left Adolph and Red 1 to compete for team leader. Adolph was tough competition, crowing the loudest, rushing aggressively towards Red and leaping up on top of any available surface—a bale of hay or a piece of farm machinery—to pronounce his dominance. He won. The hens took a vote and when Adolph crowed, they followed.

Now a grown rooster, Adolph decides for the flock where to dine on slugs, when to move on to another location, when to go into the barn and roll in the dry dirt over by the cats' bowl, and when to leap onto our picnic table and poop. In return for his flock management skills, the hens indulge Adolph's sexual urges, which is clearly, if anyone's paying attention, not the highlight of their day.

It seemed that the older Adolph got and the more power he gained, the more adverse was the effect on his personality. He seemed to be threatened by everything, including me, charging when he saw me, never quite managing to peck, but only because I would swirl around with my version of a karate kick. I would yell harshly. He would stop short of my extended boot, pose, and crow over and over until I left. He went ballistic if he caught either Chuck or Red having their way with any of the hens, and nearly went insane on the rare occasion when Chuck would mount Lucky Duck. (In this case not such an appropriate name, although she didn't actually seem to mind.) No human was beyond Adolph's ire and we all took to carrying a club when we approached him. That is, all but Jim, who greatly admired Adolph's behavior. I swear the both of them go through life with the same proportional testosterone level and, as a result, they maintain an odd poultry/human mutual admiration club.

The polarity between Jim's admiration for Adolph and my extreme dislike of Adolph began to drive a wedge between us. Jim scoffed at me for carrying the club.

My dislike turned to hatred. I refused to feed the chickens and announced that I would have nothing to do with the flock until Adolph was no longer a member. I showered my attention on the three ducks, of whom I grew very fond, and Jim and I grew distant. Jim refused to banish Adolph. He said it wasn't right to kill a rooster for doing his job well. It became hard to explain to my friends that Jim was choosing Adolph over me without feeling a vague sense of humiliation.

And then, my feelings changed, literally overnight.

It was a beautiful winter day and Unlucky Duck was just gone. No note, no feathers in a heap, no squawking — just Lucky and Helen waddling around quacking like always, except without Unlucky, whose name seemed to have a prophetic element to it. It didn't take me long to notice there were five, I counted them, five bald eagles circling the farm. I could see what they were circling... Adolph and his little band of hens, the two other roosters, and the two (remaining) ducks. The flock was oblivious to the menace and had chosen at that time to peruse the field (as in, out in the complete open and away from the barnyard buildings) for insects and slugs. They could spend all day out in the open as long as it wasn't raining, looking for food and fresh air and thriving on what we proudly claimed to our friends who bought eggs from us: the free range.

But now five eagles were circling and Unlucky had turned up missing and free range was starting to more resemble dead range when, using my trusty iPhone, Google informed me that indeed an eagle could carry off a duck, even one as healthy and plump as Unlucky.

We had a crisis. It was winter. I reasoned the eagles' regular fare of chipmunks and rats were hibernating. We would simply have to keep the chickens and ducks penned up. Lucky and Helen would not be able to meander down to our pond and take a swim at will, as they were accustomed to, but rather would be relegated to pushing themselves around the upside down garbage can lid we used as their porto-pond before we let them free range.

But our chicken pen was sub-par. This is the Pacific Northwest, with days on end of rain, and we didn't have a covered run for the chickens who, unlike the ducks, needed somewhere to escape when it poured rain. They could hang out in their coop but it was small and stuffy and full of chicken poop and then they would get diseases and be unhappy. As free rangers, once we opened the pen every morning, they made a mad dash from the stuffy coop through the downpour up into the greenhouses, rolling in the dirt and pooping up a storm, adding valuable nitrates to the soil that encouraged those county-fair-winning record-breaking beefsteak tomatoes that grew in the same building during the summer. When the rain let up, they wandered out into the field to search out earwigs and earthworms for lunch. When it hit four-thirty and the winter sun was going down, they ambled back to their chicken coop, which was a little close, as we say, and a bit stinky, but had nests and perches and all the accoutrements that chickens needed for a full life.

Lucky and Helen — and Unlucky before her unfortunate departure — were, as near as I could tell, damn good sports about it all. Ducks are much easier to manage than chickens. They don't need perches, they don't need shelter particularly since they do just fine in cold weather, they don't even need ponds, although they do love an opportunity to dunk their heads under water. They lay eggs like crazy. And they were flexible, joining in as part of Adolph's flock, even though the rest of the flock were chickens.

But now the eagles were soaring and Adolph was crowing and I feared that Lucky and Helen, not to mention Wilma and Greta and all the other hens, were at terrible risk of being carried off into the horizon to meet the same unfortunate fate as Unlucky.

Jim and I needed to act. In spite of the tension between us, we spent the entire rest of the day changing the life of the flock. We moved a little portable red chicken coop to the space between the two main greenhouses, parking it next to a doorway with the ramp stretching into the greenhouse. We pounded metal posts into the ground in the area between the houses, stretching chicken wire between so the birds could meander between the two buildings, one full of a green ground cover and the other holding the delightful dirt they loved to roll in. We staked down the chicken wire so the varmints of the woods — bobcats, raccoons, and mink — couldn't sneak their way in. We stapled plastic around the edges of the greenhouses, scouring for holes where stealthy varmints could enter. I dragged the roost up into the larger greenhouse, angling its sides out at the Y that let it stand so the birds could perch. I tied pieces of foil to the fence: the reflection was meant to frighten the eagles from landing, an optimistic idea that I found once again Googling on my iPhone. Finally I dug a small indentation in the ground where I placed Lucky and Helen's green plastic saucer. In some duck circles it might have been thought an insult, considering their prowess at diving and soaring through the water, but this was the best we could do under the circumstances.

We lured the whole team of them with chicken scratch into their new winter Club Med digs of a chicken yard. I breathed a sigh of relief as Helen and Lucky delicately climbed into their plastic garbage can lid pond and paddled around, pretending their feet weren't hitting the bottom.

That night we learned that change was not easy on flocks. Normally, they immediately trooped into the coop as the sun was setting but on this, their first night in their new home, we realized that the term "inside" was ambiguous, at best. The coop ramp was inside the greenhouse which to them was already inside and the perch I'd dragged up was also inside the greenhouse, although not inside the coop, where there was another smaller perch. Their requirement for calling it a night was to perch inside, and they spent the first night outside in (but still inside of) the greenhouse.

But chickens need more warmth than the plastic walls of our greenhouse could contain. No matter how much they huddled together, they would not be able to heat up that whole room.

Somehow they survived that night.

The next day I moved the perch outside between the greenhouses, knowing they would never spend the night out there and would figure out that they had to go inside the actual coop to the smaller perch. And, of course, Lucky and Helen would follow, hunkering down in some corner of the coop away from falling chicken poop deposited by their snoozing buddies above.

On the second night we watched as the chickens ambled their way up the ramp into the red coop, feeling certain before we set out for a dinner date that when we returned the entire flock would be neatly tucked into their poultry bed and we could gently close the little chicken-sized door (which Adolph knew to kick open in the morning) and between the fence, the greenhouse, and the red chicken house with the shut door, our flock would be safe for one more night.

At ten o'clock we returned home and, flashlight in hand, went together to shut the birds in for the night. Much to our distress, even before we entered the greenhouse, we could hear Helen quacking. Our light revealed her circling the ramp, with Lucky behind her, trying to figure out how the heck to get up the angle. Their duck feet hadn't been programmed for upward slants. They must have been trying for hours to imagine reaching the top. We flashed the light around the greenhouse which revealed no birds—the rest had managed to get inside the coop, and only the ducks were left in confusion.

And then we noticed through the vague light given off by our flashlight something perched on a pipe that was part of the greenhouse frame. There, precariously hanging onto a skinny bar that angled inches from the greenhouse wall, was Adolph. He should have been sleeping, but instead had appointed himself the nighthawk of Old Tarboo Farm, refusing to cave in to slumber before his entire flock was inside the coop. While the gap between chicken and duck language did not allow him to communicate to Helen and Lucky that all they needed to do was to walk like always, although this time in an upward angle, to arrive inside the chicken coop, he still felt his obligation to oversee them, maybe even protect them if something happened, even if all he could really do was crow and charge, which may or may not have been effective against a bobcat or coyote or mink. But, regardless of how futile his efforts might be, he was available and ready for action, even at ten at night, literally six hours after his winter bedtime.

His hens were all in, but his ducks were not, in fact, in a row, so Adolph waited outside until they were... which, as near as we could tell, took two more nights before Lucky, a Cayuga duck with her center of gravity rather low, figured out how to waddle up the ramp and Helen, a skinny, tall runner duck whose ancestors came over from Asia, learned how to walk to the base and then fly up the two feet to the top. And then they were finally inside for the night, followed by Adolph, who didn't rest until all of his girls were tucked in, even those that weren't his species.

And while on one level the utter macho of Adolph seemed so presumptuous, I couldn't help but admire him. How long each night must have seemed in the quiet eerie air of a darkened greenhouse, the chill of the night, the stars almost visible through the plastic as he stood sentry over his ducks, waiting for that plump Cayuga Lucky and her little white Indian Runner friend Helen to learn how to finally go up a ramp on a starry snowy night on the Olympic Peninsula.

We should all have such protectors.

Michael Chabon *is a renowned author and eager and active supporter of the 826 organization. His books include* The Amazing Adventures of Kavalier and Clay, The Yiddish Policemen's Union, *and* Manhood for Amateurs.

POPOVER PANCAKES

FROM *Egg Recipes from Old Tarboo Farm*

by Michael Chabon

THIS IS OUR FAVORITE "special breakfast" item. It's adapted from the recipe James Beard gives in his *American Cookery* (my favorite cookbook) for the German pancakes served by Henry Thiele's, a sadly defunct old-time Portland, Oregon restaurant I remember from its final days in the late eighties. Beard says to do it in a skillet, then when it's done, roll it up like a cigar. But I use two cake pans and serve them all puffed up and glorious. Plus, I add vanilla and use powdered sugar to glaze it. Serves 4.

INGREDIENTS

1 cup flour
2 teaspoons salt
3 tablespoons sugar
1 cup cream
½ teaspoon vanilla
9 eggs

4 tablespoons butter
powdered sugar
lemon juice

DIRECTIONS

Preheat oven to 400 degrees. Mix first five ingredients into a smooth paste. Add the eggs, one at a time, beating each in before continuing. Split the butter between two 9-inch cake pans and stick in oven to melt the butter. Divide the batter between the two pans of melted butter. Bake until they get mountainous and spectacular, about 15-20 minutes. Sprinkle with powdered sugar, squeeze on lemon juice. Mmm.

David Gonzalez *likes the Atlanta Falcons and learning things. He wrote this recipe when he was in third grade, but he is much older and wiser now.*

HAMBURGER RAIN

FROM *826 Seattle Writes the Rain*

by David Gonzalez

THE STORY OF THIS RECIPE: In the summer it rains hamburgers—but only in Seattle! In the winter it rains water. It rains hamburgers only in the summer because then they will get cooked by the sun. If you want a cheeseburger, just think about it and the cheese will be on the burger!

INGREDIENTS: Hamburger rain, mayonnaise, ketchup, crispy chicken, lettuce, buns

TOOLS: A plate

DIRECTIONS: Catch the hamburgers with the plate when they fall from the sky. Enjoy eating them with the rest of the ingredients.

Kathleen Alcalá *is the author of five books set in the Southwestern United States and Mexico. Her most recent work,* Desert Remembers My Name, *was published in 2007. When it rains, she likes to read travel books, walk to the post office, and curl up with her cat while drinking green tea and eating pistachios. Alcalá was recently named an island treasure by the Arts and Humanities Council on Bainbridge Island, where she lives.*

SWEET LIFE

by Kathleen Alcalá

BAINBRIDGE ISLAND CURLS like a fist of rock around Eagle Harbor on the western edge of Puget Sound, thirty-five minutes from downtown Seattle by ferry. More than half the working population commutes to Seattle every day on a Jumbo Mark II, either the *Tacoma* or the *Wenatchee*. The ferries resemble floating airports, they are so large and stable: each is capable of carrying 2,500 passengers and 200 vehicles at a time.

Once in a while, the placid waters of Puget Sound are rough enough that a ferry is cancelled, and people must wait for the next one. Or the boat is held at the island for an ambulance taking a critical patient to one of the hospitals in Seattle. Otherwise, they must be airlifted by helicopter. One must be patient to live on an island. Off the northwest corner of Bainbridge is the short Agate Point Bridge, leading to the Kitsap Peninsula and all points west. Agate Pass used to be crossed by a small private ferry, and a few old-timers remember rousing the ferryman to take them home early in the morning after a night out.

I have joked that, if we were completely cut off from the mainland, Bainbridge Island, with its population of about 25,000, could live off of locally made white wine and goat cheese for quite awhile. Every April the farmer's market reopens, and we have our choice of goat cheese, honey, and a few vegetables. The truth is, our growing season is short, and there are just some things that won't grow here in quantity. The soil is bad, and the local gardening guru, Ann Lovejoy, recommends buying good soil and dumping it directly on top, rather than attempting to work it into the rocky hardpan that dominates the terrain.

But also, members of the farmer's market protect their own interests. Products must be grown or made within Kitsap County, and farmers must be approved by the board. The owner of an old produce stand near the highway no longer grows food but, a few years ago, tried to import produce from Eastern Washington to sell at the convenient spot. Members of the farmer's market got it shut down as a violation of their regulations.

As a result, most of our produce is still purchased through the locally owned Town and Country Market and a Safeway store. Once, Bainbridge was famous for its strawberries, but a blight, along with the forced internment of Japanese American farmers during World War II, ended their production. By the fall, a greater variety is available, but as Americans, we are used to having seasonal products year-round: lettuce, tomatoes, broccoli, avocados, citrus fruits, things that grow in limited quantities or not at all in our cool, wet climate. "There are no seasons in the American supermarket," according to the movie, *Food, Inc.* (2008).

Bob and Nancy Fortner, who I first knew as booksellers, now sell honey, soap, skin care products, and preserves, all produced at Sweetlife Farm, at the farmer's market. This is from their website:

> Sweetlife Farm is a "cottage" business (just the two of us); we value quality over quantity, and urge you to purchase as things appeal to you, understanding that everything is a "limited edition," and may not be available again.

"We try to grow enough to feed ourselves and make value-added products," says Nancy. It is all made in their Department of Agriculture-certified kitchen.

This is not the first transformation the Fortners have made. They met as medical professionals at the William Beaumont Army Medical Center in El Paso, Texas. They married and moved to the Bay area, where they lived in a house high in La Honda, and Bob practiced nephrology at El Camino Hospital. Bob and Nancy moved to Washington state in 1992, where Bob was born, and he continued to practice medicine part time, until he eventually became disillusioned with the profession.

"The changing ethics of the medical profession," he says, "contributed to the fragmentation of medical care." As doctor's groups tried to reorganize as businesses, he felt patient priorities taking second place: "When the pie gets smaller, the table manners change."

Sweetlife Farm is on one of the highest points on the island, maybe three hundred feet above sea level. It often snows here when it does not snow at my house, which is about a hundred feet above the cold waters of Eagle Harbor.

In the winter, the steep, gabled roofs shelter the entrances to their Arts and Crafts style home, and to the building that now houses their commercial kitchen and show room. "Christmas in the Country" is an island-wide event that encourages shoppers to travel from one venue to another, "buying local," and the Fortners always host several artists whose wares complement their own seasonal products such as "Cocoa Local" and Nancy's meticulously wrapped gift soaps.

"The evolution of none of this was planned," Bob says. "There are early decisions, early influences under which you fall." One was the writings of Helen and Scott Nearing. In 1954 they published *Living the Good Life*. Bob and Nancy discovered it in the 1970s. The book advocated a "back to the land" lifestyle, and described how the Nearings grew most of their food on a farm in Vermont. After Scott Nearing was kicked out of academia for being a Communist during the Depression, the book recounts how the two of them were able to sustain themselves with almost nothing purchased from the outside, while leaving half of the year free to travel and promulgate their ideas. "Such a handbook," says the preface, "is needed for the many individuals and families, tied to city jobs and dwellings, who yearn to make their dreams of the good life a reality."

A follow-up book "by that frugal housewife" Helen Nearing, *Simple Food for the Good Life* (1980), includes recipes and a description of the kind of food they grew and ate, such as "Casseroled Carrots" and "Buckwheat Crunchies."

The Fortners did much of the work themselves in building their present house, with its view across a small pond to a natural stream, backed by hundred-year-old Douglas firs. Every time I go over there, it seems, a new structure has been added. At the last Christmas in the Country, a wood-fired oven had been added, in a cute little shingled building covered in tiny Christmas lights. A florist was exhibiting in there, and I worried for the first time that Sweetlife Farm was beginning to resemble those commercial gardens that rely as much on tourists as on regular customers. Was this a proprietary feeling? If I feel that way, it is because the Fortners have cultivated that feeling in a great many people. I think of the Fortner's house as the island's living room. Although this is a small town, it is a big island, the size of Manhattan, and we do not cross paths that often. By providing a place for intentional gathering, either for work or play, the Fortners have strengthened the fabric of our community.

I decided that if there is ever a major emergency, such as the bridge washing away and the ferry service shut down indefinitely, I will make my way to the Fortners'. I'm not sure how they feel about that. But I know that if I showed up under those circumstances, they would put me right to work. I have never seen either of the Fortners—Nancy, sixty-two, and Bob, seventy—compact, energetic people, idle.

I continued to think about those ideas, the what-ifs implied by people trying to become independent of the grocery store for their food. I have some other friends, Marilyn Holt and her husband Cliff Wind, who run a farm in South Kitsap County. I decide to introduce these people to each other and start asking some of my questions.

On a Thursday morning, Nancy and I followed the directions to Holt Ranch. Bob had already left for a sustainable farming meeting in Port Townsend. Forty-five minutes later, Marilyn and Cliff and their three dogs welcomed us inside, where we gathered around their dining room table. The oilcloth had a rooster design, and Marilyn served strong coffee.

The current farmhouse was built in about 1900. It is the second house on the spot, and the third on the property. The first was at the top of a small rise, partly underground. A new house was built when the spring ran dry, but the present location, near a creek, is too wet. Marilyn's great-grandfather, Frederick Walker, bought the farm in 1892 from the homesteaders, Mr. and Mrs. Cooksey.

Cliff retired in October of last year. He had worked for the United States Postal Service since 1977, unable to find a position teaching math and science. He spent two years teaching in Australia, but still couldn't find a teaching job when he returned.

Marilyn worked as a technical writer and became a certified management consultant. From 1999 to 2000 she was the chief financial officer of an e-book company. She still has a consulting company, Holt Capital, and says she may return to it in a year or two. I know Marilyn as one of the founders of Clarion West, a science fiction writers' workshop, and she has an authoritative air that would make young software developers pay attention.

In late 1998 or early 1999, it became obvious, says Marilyn, that her father needed help with the farm. Her mother had died in 1982, and Marilyn is an only child. When Marilyn took over, she was simply considering which five acres to sell in order to pay for his care. He had Alzheimer's and MRSA—methicillin-resistant staphylococcus aureus, a bacterial infection common in hospitals. The cost for his care was "amazing."

"I didn't think I'd get it," she says of the farm.

Marilyn and Cliff have one permanent, part-time employee, and last summer hired sixteen teenagers part time, between the ages of fourteen and eighteen. Because it is hard labor, a different set of employment rules apply for hiring young people. For example, no one under sixteen can drive any of their farm equipment.

"I'm a huge 'right to farm' advocate," Marilyn says, meaning she opposes regulations that restrict farming close to high-density areas. In communities like ours, this can be an issue as urban areas begin to impinge on rural areas, or cities try to conform to the statewide Growth Management Act, which mandates planning for increased density. It does not look like an issue at Marilyn's farm, which is surrounded by other small farms and houses with a few acres. Still, if someone nearby decided to subdivide their property into lots and build houses, there could be complaints about the odors associated with raising cattle, or the noise of farm equipment.

Marilyn tells me what seeds she had bought for the coming season: lettuce, broccoli, onions, garlic, beets, carrots, bok choy, kohlrabi, potatoes, beans, and corn. They plan to put seven acres in crops, and keep twenty in pasture for the cattle. A lot of the vegetables will be started under plastic.

"We do a lot out of books," says Cliff.
Marilyn agrees. "The knowledge has been lost. We need to find it in books."

They consult the books of a farmer in Maine who uses unheated greenhouses. According to the website for Four Season Farm (www.fourseasonfarm.com), it is "an experimental market garden in Harborside, Maine, owned and operated by writers Barbara Damrosch and Elliott

Coleman. The farm produces vegetables year-round and has become a nationally recognized model of small-scale sustainable agriculture." The photos show clean, spacious greenhouses with wide rows of orderly vegetables and enough vertical space to grow corn. It looks like something out of the space movie *Logan's Run*.

Both couples farm full-time. At first, Marilyn and Cliff focused on hay and cattle. About four years ago, Holt Ranch became a CSA, or Community Supported Agriculture, farm, which means that individual families pay at the beginning of each season to receive a share of produce. Under the name "Abundantly Green," Holt Ranch begins its CSA season on June 1, and continues through September. This model has grown increasingly popular across the country over the last twenty years. The advantage to farmers is that they receive cash up front. Consumers receive fresh, locally grown produce, forming a relationship with a specific farm and its products. The beef, which is organic but not certified, in order to save on cost, is already gone for the season.

Otherwise, Cliff and Marilyn sell at the Poulsbo Farmer's Market, and distribute their CSA shares in Poulsbo, Port Orchard, and at the farm. Outside, Cliff and Marilyn show off a bright yellow cart built by her cousin for use at the market. It has bins and drawers that open out to display the vegetables. The farmer's market is Cliff's realm. He staffs the market stall during the season, and distributes the CSA shares, a rotating variety of vegetables as the season progresses, to participating families.

I ask the hypothetical question that sent me on this quest: If there was a food emergency, and I showed up and wanted to work for food, what would they have me do?

"We can all do something," Marilyn says. "Weed. I would expect you to learn how to field dress." This means to slaughter an animal and divide the meat into its appropriate parts for consumption. Basic gardening, she says: loosening the soil, harvesting vegetables, seed saving. Marilyn, it turns out, cannot touch the ground: she is allergic to mold, as well as much of the produce that they grow, such as legumes. She describes putting a bean into her mouth but having to spit it out as her throat began to swell.

Marilyn's mother used to read *The Little Red Book: Quotations from Chairman Mao* with her, and tell her to keep the farm for when the Revolution came. This made me wish I could have interviewed Marilyn's mother.

With herself now fifty-nine, and Cliff fifty-seven, Marilyn noted that they are the national average for farmers in the United States. Cliff never expected to end up a farmer. He likes the interaction with CSA shareholders, "interesting folks doing this for different reasons." Often, they do not know how to prepare the food.

We pulled on our mud boots and went outside in the drizzle. I was the only one using an umbrella. Marilyn and Cliff showed us the two big greenhouses where they planned to put starts. As I crouched to look inside the long canvas tunnels, I saw that they were set directly on the ground, and full of mud and weeds. They were about four feet tall, and workers would have to crawl or crouch to plant or weed in them. We walked by a large barn, built from a Sears kit around 1930. It occurred to me that the beautiful weathered planks on the barn are probably worth more than the building itself.

Another outbuilding contained cold storage units for their produce in the summer. This looked relatively new, and Cliff and Marilyn seemed very happy with it. The extra storage will enable them to harvest food for the CSA shares ahead of time and prepare the boxes on the spot. We passed an area full of old tractors and their attachments, the sorts of farm vehicles that preceded combines. The farm is the kind of place my husband would call "Implement City" when we lived in Western Colorado—farmers have no way of disposing of outdated or obsolete equipment, so it usually just rusts in piles around the property.

Cliff, a thin man with a long, graying ponytail, held up a stray kohlrabi from the previous season and, with a wizard's flourish, did a little presentation on this root vegetable. I saw what a great math and science teacher he would have made. He told us the best way to eat it is steamed, mashed, and served like mashed potatoes. I've been to potlucks with Cliff and Marilyn, and Cliff is the one who dares exotic fruits and vegetables.

Farther east towards the pasture, we carefully climbed over an electric fence. The smallest dog had come with us, and had to be lifted over. While we stood and surveyed the property—which runs slightly uphill from west, where a creek borders the property, to east—Marilyn said that, when the land is under cultivation, it can yield $1,000 worth of produce per acre a week. All I saw was damp pasture where the cattle grazed north of us, mud where we stood. I wondered if, given their overhead, this was sustainable. Granted, Kitsap County in February, most farms are probably fallow. But when I asked Nancy about it later, she said most CSA farmers had their starts in the greenhouse by then.

We walked up a rise to the site of the original farmhouse. The stumps of old hazelnut trees mark the spot, which looks south across open land to dark forest beyond, and is flanked on the east by firs and pines. It's a beautiful setting, and I wondered what it had looked like to Marilyn's great-grandfather when he first laid eyes on it.

I asked Cliff and Marilyn how they envision their farm in thirty years. Will it still be a farm? "I hope so," says Marilyn. "Yes, I see it as still being a farm." Marilyn has faith that, as long as people know how to work the land, there will be sustainable agriculture. On Bainbridge, there is a man who grows wine grapes and talks a lot about terroir, a French term for the characteristics of a specific piece of land. Cliff and Marilyn have invested in the terroir of Holt Ranch, and believe that specific knowledge can and will be passed on to others.

Driving back to Bainbridge, Nancy explained that the Fortners work their small farm with only one field mower. Nine of the ten acres are in a land trust, to remain undeveloped. In the summers, they hire a man from Mexico named Saúl to mow. This year, Nancy and Bob converted more of their property to active production, and Saúl will take home half for his family. Saúl welcomed the idea, because he and his family, who he does not see that much because of his numerous jobs, will help.

"When I leave this house," Nancy has said, "they're going to have to carry me out feet first." They are building a small cottage to move Nancy's parents here from Mississippi. It is hard to say if any of Bob and Nancy's three grown children will continue the business, since the Fortners followed many roads before coming to this place.

I realized that the practical questions I had come with—how many acres, elevations, how many days of sunlight—were not as important as the question I thought might be the most frivolous: if I were desperate, what could I do to earn food? I wasn't thinking of a Cormac McCarthy scenario, like *The Road*, as much as a breakdown in transportation, since almost all of our food is shipped or trucked in. The most important factor in the equation turns out to be simply labor: The more hours a human being works on a farm, the more it can produce.

"We have not solved the problem of living," wrote the Nearings. "Far from it. But our experience convinces us that no family group possessing a normal share of vigor, energy, purpose, imagination and determination need to continue to wear the yoke of competitive, acquisitive, predatory culture."

Marilyn, Cliff, Nancy, and Bob have not solved the problem of living. But if they succeed in finding and maintaining the sweet life, we will all benefit. There is always earth. And around here, there is always water. As long as there are people who need to eat, and people who have preserved the knowledge of growing food, we will be willing to work.

175

Famed Seattle chef **Tom Douglas** *is owner of six restaurants and a bakery, author of three cookbooks, most recently* Tom's Big Dinners, *and makes a salmon rub that lives up to the reputation of the Northwest's iconic fish. He even has his own Amazon.com tool line. When he's not wowing eaters, he keeps busy supporting local farmers.*

LORETTA'S BUTTERMILK PANCAKES WITH WILD BLACKBERRIES

FROM *Tom Douglas' Seattle Kitchen*

by Tom Douglas

MY DAUGHTER, LORETTA, and I have many breakfast traditions. Some are exotic, like dim sum, where we battle each other for the tiny lup chong (Chinese sausage) buried deep inside the lotus leaf wrapped Nor Mai Gai sticky rice ball, while others are simple, like griddling Norwegian lefse slathered in butter and sprinkled with fresh grinds of black pepper and sea salt until golden brown and crispy.

When cooking breakfast at home in Seattle, we have a fabulous breakfast ingredient right in our backyard. Wild blackberries grow like ferocious weeds in backyards, along freeways, and most anywhere you really don't want them. When I get tired of whacking them down, sometimes I stop to pick a few to have with these pancakes.

Loretta likes silver dollar-size pancakes, but you can make them larger if you like.

INGREDIENTS

3 cups all-purpose flour
1 tablespoon sugar
1½ teaspoons baking soda
1½ teaspoons kosher salt
1 teaspoon baking powder
2 large eggs
3½ cups buttermilk
¼ cup (½ stick) unsalted butter, melted, plus more for serving
Pure maple syrup
1 pint fresh blackberries, or other berries

DIRECTIONS

In a bowl, sift together the flour, sugar, baking soda, salt, and baking powder. In another bowl, combine the eggs and buttermilk, then add the melted butter. Gradually add the wet to the dry ingredients, stirring with a wooden spoon until just smooth. Heat a nonstick griddle over medium-high heat. Drop the batter by the ¼ cupful (or, if you want to make the tiny silver dollar pancakes Loretta likes, drop the batter by the tablespoonful) into the hot pan and cook until they are full of bubbles and the bottom side is golden (lift the pancake with a spatula to check the bottom), 2 to 3 minutes. Flip and cook the other side, about 1 more minute.

Serve these pancakes with melted butter and maple syrup along with a bowl of the blackberries.

Makes 6 servings.

Myla Goldberg *is the best selling author of* Wickett's Remedy *and* The Bee Season. *She is "disturbingly" double jointed and can sometimes taste things in her dreams. Her favorite place in the Northwest when it rains is New York; Goldberg has only ever lived in the Northwest during the summer. Her most recent novel,* The False Friend, *will be released in October 2010. She currently lives in Brooklyn with her husband and their daughter.*

SALMON WITH GRAPES

by *Myla Goldberg*

AFTER MY SOPHOMORE year of college, I spent the summer in Seattle, painting houses. At the end of the day, I'd be so exhausted that dinner often consisted of spooning peanut butter and marshmallow fluff into my mouth straight from their jars. I'm not even sure I knew the relationship between salmon and the Northwest that summer, only that I pined for my Mom's cooking and especially this salmon recipe. It is ridiculously easy to make and has converted many of the self-professed fish-shy to avid salmon-eaters. I generally use more grapes than the recipe calls for, because they're so delicious. I prefer the sharpness of red grapes here, though the mellower green grape works too.

INGREDIENTS

40 ounces of salmon, fillets or steaks
1 tablespoon butter
1 teaspoon salt
¼ teaspoon pepper
3 tablespoons finely chopped shallot or onion
½ cup dry red wine
Juice of ½ lemon
½ teaspoon cornstarch dissolved in 1 tablespoon cold water
½ cup seedless grapes, halved

DIRECTIONS

Pre-heat oven to 400 degrees. Melt butter in baking pan, then coat salmon on both sides. Season with salt and pepper. Bake for 5 minutes, uncovered. Combine shallots, wine, and lemon juice in small saucepan. Simmer for 5 minutes over medium heat. Stir dissolved cornstarch into sauce to thicken. Pour sauce over fish. Add grapes and bake for 10 minutes more.

Oliver Cauble *has been a student at 826 Seattle for two years, during which he has learned more than he ever thought possible about commas and periods. His favorite food is mac'n'cheese, followed closely with s'mores. He's not quite sure what he wants to be when he grows up, but he wants it to be fun.*

THE S'MORE-TAINOUS MONSTER

FROM *When a Sentence Ends in a Surprising Gazebo*

by Oliver Cauble

SOMETHING WAS BURNING in the oven. It was a marshmallow that suddenly (Do! Do! Doo!) ran away because it was hot. Then a storm came by and the marshmallow got struck by lightning. It made it all crisp and yummy—and evil! It began to grow as tall as a house.

Two kids named Conrad and Sally saw the marshmallow. They were surprised, but mostly they were excited about making a giant s'more with it. Conrad and Sally ran home and got two big graham crackers and a chocolate bar. They ran after the marshmallow for hours. They were pretty smart kids, and they had made their own robotic arms to carry heavy things, so they were able to keep running.

The marshmallow didn't see Conrad and Sally at first. It was just running to try to cool down, because the lightning made it hot. The marshmallow climbed the Space Needle, and Conrad and Sally followed it. Neither of them had had a s'more in so long; they wanted the giant marshmallow so badly they didn't even pay attention to how scary it was to climb the Space Needle. The weather was still stormy and the marshmallow got struck by lightning again. It was so swollen now, it started to float up to space.

Conrad and Sally grabbed onto its leg and they were heavy enough to drag it back down. Sally dropped a graham cracker and Conrad dropped the chocolate bar. They fell for twenty seconds, and the marshmallow landed on top of the chocolate bar. Sally and Conrad put the second graham cracker on top and started jumping on it to squish the marshmallow down. And then they ate it! They put their leftovers in a ginormous plastic bag and dragged them home for later.

FORECAST: Cats and Dogs

Three things that eleven-and-a-half-year-old **Mustafa Ahmed** *considers important are writing, soccer, and his father. His sister inspires him, and his friends like that he is funny. Mustafa was born in Aden, Yemen and speaks Arabic, English, and Somali. He dreams of becoming a doctor, and he'd also like you to know that he likes cats.*

I WILL WAIT FOR YOU

FROM *Having Them Here...*

by *Mustafa Ahmed*

IN MY HOUSE, there's a chair in which no one is allowed to sit. It's my dad's favorite chair. When he's away at work, my baby sister sits on the chair. If someone else sits on it, she yells, "That's my dad's chair!" My dad said, "I'm the only one who can sit in it."

My dad works on a cargo ship. He goes to Alaska, where he stays for three months at a time. When he is on the cargo ship he has to carry heavy boxes and do repairs on the ship. When he is finished with his work, he goes fishing. Sometimes he says that he likes his job, sometimes not! When he's gone, I miss him. It's hard for me to wait three months for him to come home.

He buys me almost everything that I want. He is so quiet when we are with him. But if there are some people outside of our family, he talks with them. He is short like me, and he looks like me too. My mom tells me that I do things like my dad.

My dad likes computers. He also likes to fix things.

If anything breaks, he won't wait. He will fix it right away. One day I was helping my dad make something that looked like a triangle box for our garage. When I was passing the nail to my dad, he looked at me and hit his hand really hard. My dad told me to go tell my mom. I went to tell my mom what happened. My mom brought him the first aid box.

I miss my dad when he's gone for three months. I miss him because he helps me with my homework. I miss him because he's not there to play with me! I miss him because I am not able to talk to him.

I try to keep myself busy with my games, or going outside to play with other people. If I sit and think about him, I will be sadder. When my dad is home, he plays soccer or basketball with me. We watch movies. He takes me to GameStop to buy me video games. When I ask my mom to let me go outside she says, "No." I think she say no because she's protective of me. But when I ask my dad he lets me go! My mom respects my dad. She also does everything my dad asks of her. If she wants to go somewhere she asks my dad, and when my dad is away, she stays at home. Whenever my dad is home it always feels like I have my whole family together! That's when I am happy.

Po Bronson *lives in San Francisco but he grew up in Seattle, and now spends his summers on Vashon Island. He does much of his writing in a closet where he has authored six bestsellers, both fiction and non-fiction, including* What Should I Do With My Life? *and, most recently,* NurtureShock. *When it rains, he likes to read the* New York Times, *the* Wall Street Journal *and the local paper.*

THE IMPOSSIBLE TO KILL ME GAME

FROM *Writer's Harvest 3*

by Po Bronson

THIS IS HOW WE LIVED: the year my mother met Michael, she and a friend owned a used bookstore near the Pike Place Market in Seattle, and after school I rode the 32 James downtown to help her shelve boxes of donated books and pester the panhandlers until they moved from the entrance-way. It wasn't much of a store — I had to go to the Vietnamese restaurant next door to use the bathroom — but Mom made enough money to cover mortgage payments and buy us new shoes every eight months. Mom encouraged me to read, but I faked it by memorizing the descriptions on the jackets and copying any drawings that were inside. We closed at six and took the 11 Madison home, getting off to buy dinner at Dick's Fast Food, where we ate in time to catch the next bus. We split up and stood in both lines to get to the window faster, winking at each other when the servers told the man in front of me that they didn't make fish sandwiches and couldn't take the catsup off his cheeseburger. Mom loved hot fudge sundaes and ate only those, while I hauled home a bag of six burgers and french fries for my older brother and me.

Ron was a sophomore at the high school and that winter had basketball after school until five-thirty. He played football in the fall, basketball in the winter, and track in the spring, in which he threw the javelin, but he was no bigshot teenager—he never went out on dates and didn't even own any albums. Girls didn't call at night, and he didn't go out with friends. Instead he listened to the radio a lot and couldn't fall asleep without it on. He listened to the late-night talk shows where people called in to talk about their sexual problems. At six foot four, he was so skinny that Mom still bought his belts and underwear in the boys' department. He wore leg weights strapped to his ankles and every day practiced jumping behind our house—he would jump as high as he could and soon as he landed take off again. He did this in the dark after he got home. He had read about the training in *Sports Illustrated*, and to my knowledge it worked; fifty times in a row, then a two-minute rest. Ten sets a night. He could reverse-dunk a basketball.

Ron bragged to me that he would be sixteen soon and would drive to Montana by himself that summer, despite the fact that we had no car. Our grandparents lived in Missoula, and he wanted to drive the hay truck and herd cows on their range. In three months, he would gain fifty pounds and five years of experience, come back with hair on his face and muscles on his bones. Or maybe not return at all—get a job with the state game warden and spend his days in the mountains chasing poachers and counting grizzlies.

We had a game that we played, the Impossible to Kill Me Game. Ron would invent a situation in which I was sure to die, and I would invent ways to save myself. He would slowly increase the impossibility of saving myself, and I would become more and more inventive. "I've pushed you off a cliff," he would say. "You're falling toward jagged rocks below."

"Before I fall, I flip around and grab your shoelaces," I would say.

"You can't hang by my shoelaces," he would argue. "Your fingers couldn't grip that hard."

"I could if I had to save my life. Unless you've been there, you can't say I wouldn't be especially strong."

"Then I would hit your hands with rocks until you fell."

"The cliff is slightly sloped. I would crash through bushes growing on its side until I was going slow enough to stop myself."

"No, the cliff is a cliff of cement. There's no bushes growing." He would begin to get angry, as if I was cheating. I would begin to laugh, which would only make him angrier.

"I'm carrying a huge umbrella," I would say. "I open it and float to the rocks."

"They're jagged rocks. You weren't listening."

"So maybe I break both legs. Maybe I break both legs and wrench both knees, but I'm still alive."

Mom let us know that life in the city was not easy, and the rain and the cold did not make it any easier. She often said her lungs were better suited to California.

To make it a little easier for her, Mom had a few rules. We had to take the garbage out every night, so the kitchen wouldn't smell like french fries in the morning. She wouldn't let us turn up the thermostat, but because she didn't get up in the morning until just after we had left for school, we abused this rule with a fifteen-minute tropical blast. Most of all, Mom screamed if she had to take a cold shower. Our water heater was small, could only keep two showers' worth of warm water, so when I turned twelve she made Ron shower at night. He'd been taking morning showers for three years, and it was my turn. As a result, he went to bed with his hair wet and woke up with it molded into awkward sculpture. A wet comb never seemed to bring it back to normal, and I envisioned my brother being known at the high school as the skinny boy with the uneven hair.

Michael was Mom's boyfriend. Ten years before, he had written a memoir about growing up in Tacoma a second-generation Greek immigrant. But he couldn't write anything more after that, and instead sold men's suits at a downtown department store on commission. He didn't have any kids but had been married once. He told us that he had lost all his body hair after his divorce, and this seemed strange because he was a hairy man, with bushy black curls on his head, eyebrows, and forearms. When he ate dinner with us, I sat across from him and squinted my eyes and tried to make the hair go away. Mom had met him in line at Dick's Fast Food. He had a studio apartment near there. I was with her. She recognized him, she had seen his picture on his book in her store. When we had our food, we sat down together on the orange plastic benches outside Dick's, and twice Michael gave me money for scoops of double-mint ice cream. At school that day I had learned about centrifugal motion—it's how we get the water off the lettuce—and I demonstrated the principle for him by swinging around a pole. We missed three buses. When we got home, Ron was already out back jumping into the darkness, and his hamburgers were cold. I watched him from the window, silently counting sets with him, listening to the scuff of his shoes as he fought the five-pound lead sacks belted to his ankles. Thirty-two. Thirty-three. I could hear his high-school coach in the background, Frank McCuskey, who taught history war by war and was old enough to have fought in several, warning Ron that hands on the hips between sets was a sign of weakness. Forty-eight. Forty-nine. Forty-nine and a half. Fifty.

A few weeks after the night at Dick's, Mom and I went to West Seattle for one of Michael's soccer games, where he played on a team with fellow Greeks. We went straight from the store, transferring from the 5 Central to the 42 Alki down by the Rainier brewery; she had invited Ron, too, but he lied and said he had a history paper due.

The game was in a small outdoor stadium under the lights. I knew nothing about this strange European sport, but Michael's team had silky royal blue uniforms with skull-and-crossbones patches on the shoulder. It couldn't have been more than a few degrees above freezing, but these men braved it with only baggy shorts and tall socks. Michael played somewhere on defense, and when he stole the ball he gave it a great kick down the field, toward the other end. That his kicks went right to the other team's defenders didn't matter; everyone else was knocking the ball in tight little passes, while Michael's kicks soared fifty yards, and I assumed he was the strongest on the field. I imagined bringing him to the school yard for a kickball game and watching him send the red rubber ball into orbit.

Mom sat beside me, her face white despite the winter cold, completely silent until halftime, when she let out a huge breath that she seemed to have held for the entire period. I was used to this, though, it was the same way she watched Ron at his basketball games. Her silence was a constant prayer. Sometimes I would catch her whispering to herself. She feared for her men in these situations; they could make a mistake and cost their team the game, or they could tangle up legs and ankles and get them broken. She never objected to sports and always went to our games, because she knew we needed support. But they scared her. All those men in one place.

During the tiny breaths that followed, where she brought oxygen back to her lungs and blood back to her face, I took advantage of this weakness and hit her up for popcorn and hot-dog money. We didn't have much money, but the entrance of Michael into our lives distracted us. I ate the dog and the popcorn before I could make it back to my seat, so I turned around and went back for more. I was always hungry when it was cold. Mom took a single bite with her front teeth from the back end of my hot dog. She was dieting, she said.

The second half began. Mom started to talk then.

"You have to get used to them not scoring much," she said. "There's a fine appreciation to this sport. They don't have cheerleaders and halftime shows."

"I like it," I answered. It was a men's game, clearly, and I'm not sure Mom could appreciate it fully herself.

"Someday you'll travel, Lou. Someday you'll go places and learn about what they do in other countries."

"In Greece they drink lots of wine, I know that. And eat olives."

"Michael told you that?"

"Sure." But he hadn't, and he didn't need to. It was intuitive. Salty cheese, sexy women, old men in overalls and little caps working the fields. It was better than Montana. It beat Montana hands down.

"I'm glad Michael can share with you," she said then. It's important to me."

There was a corner kick. Michael came up from the back to stand at the rear of the crowd and then rushed in just as his teammate booted the ball hard and straight into the mob of players. Michael ran straight at the ball and got his head on it, flicking it backward, over the top of the goalie and into the far side of the net. With his head! I thought they might call it back because he didn't kick it in, but he kept on running right past the goal and then in a big circle back onto the field at full sprint with his arms high over his head. I knew then that Michael was in our future, and it seemed impossible that he hadn't been my real father all along. His teammates lifted him off the ground and tried to carry him several yards, but their legs gave way and they all spilled to the ground. I was in my seat with my arms over my head.

Mom let out another breath, and this one led into silent crying, which she disguised by reknotting her scarf around her neck at the same time. She asked if I was hungry again. She took my hot-dog napkin and blew her nose. She straightened her wool hat.

This is what Michael and my mother would do at night: they would get out a bottle of wine, sit around the table, and talk. For years I had asked to be excused as soon as I could finish the last of my peas or french fries. Mom never minded, because Ron and I would only argue at the table anyway, or play Impossible to Kill Me, or shave off our calluses with a steak knife. Ron would brag about how long he could keep his finger in a candle flame, and I would challenge him, and then we would argue over whether he had counted too fast. But then, when Michael appeared, I suddenly wanted to stay at the table and listen to their talk. Michael convinced my mother that a shot glass of wine every few days wouldn't hurt a twelve-year old. Michael always brought copies of magazines with him, for my mother to read a fascinating article he'd found, and they would discuss it together. While they talked, I copied the little drawings that were tucked in at the bottoms of the pages.

I liked to hear my mother's voice with a man's, talking, two voices in a dining room, and sometimes I got so relaxed I fell asleep in my chair. When I woke, it would be close to midnight, the lights would be dimmed, the portable radio would be tapping out a light jazz tune, and Michael would be waltzing my mother across the kitchen floor. For a while I would pretend to still be asleep, but when they started kissing I would go upstairs quietly, and I would hear Ron's radio, more talk shows. I would open the door to his room and very slowly turn down the sound to nothing. I would stand over Ron's bed and watch him sleep. Sometimes I reached out and touched his hair, which was still just slightly damp, hours after showering.

A couple of Saturdays later, Mom sent us down to Michael's department store for new suits. The store had a sale, and it was time, as Mom told us when we walked out the door, to dress the part of the young men we were quickly becoming. It was early February. It had snowed more the night before, and in the streets this had melted and refrozen into invisible ice patches. Our crowded bus kept getting stuck on the hill, and we had to get out to lighten the load and walk to the bus stop ahead, then get back on. By this time we had lost our seats, and since I couldn't reach the overhead railings, I hung on to Ron's parka. He kept jerking it away from my grip and I tried to stand for a while, but as the bus lurched I stumbled and reached out for his parka on the way down. From the floor I noticed he has his leg weights on. When Ron picked me up, he said, "Okay, stop that," like a parent and it made me laugh. When I wouldn't stop laughing, he started in on a scenario.

"You're taped into a seat on a bus. Big wide strips of that gray tape they use for pipes. You're the only one on the bus, and the bus is headed down an icy hill without any brakes. At the bottom of the hill is a brick wall."

"That wouldn't kill me. I would be protected by the frame of the bus."

"Yes, it would. The bus would crunch up like an accordion, with you in it."

"Then my faithful dog Sparks chews me free of the tape, and I rush to the wheel of the bus and steer it down a side road."

"You don't have a dog. You haven't had a dog since Teddy died when you were six."

I lied. "Michael's going to get me one for my birthday. He told me."

"This is before your birthday. This is right now."

"Then I've been eating these special seeds that make my saliva able to dissolve any glue, and I spit on the tape to free myself."

"That would take too long."

"I work very fast under pressure."

"Then I've chloroformed you before taping you in.

PO BRONSON

THE IMPOSSIBLE TO KILL ME GAME

You're unconscious."

"I only look unconscious. I'm faking it. These special seeds also make me immune to chloroform. In fact, not only do I avert disaster, but I drive the bus all the way to Montana."

"No way, you'd be dead."

"I'd be a game warden. I'd be arresting poachers." I think he would have hit me if the bus hadn't been full of witnesses. But soon it was our stop, and once off the bus we gave up arguing. Ron walked ahead of me, as if he didn't want anyone to think we were brothers. Once he turned around and warned me not to touch anything when we got in the store. None of this mattered to me. A doorman swung the great gold doors open for us, and then I smelled the warm air and the perfume that all the dressed-up ladies were spraying onto themselves. I considered stealing a small bottle for Mom, but she would know I had stolen it, so I kept my hands in my pockets until I got to men's suits.

The walls were covered in dark shiny wood, and the carpeting was so thick that I didn't make any sound when I walked. Glass cases of ties circled the room. Michael had told me about the ties — no two the same. I looked carefully, checking his assertion, trying to find two that were identical. Then Michael found us. He helped us off with our coats as if we were regular clients, then went to measuring us, down our inseams, around our waists and chests. He whistled when he measured Ron's shirt sleeve. Ron's arms were extra long; they could almost reach his knees, like a gorilla.

"I'll have a hard time fitting you two," he said. He got on the phone, called downstairs, and asked for someone to bring up a blue suit in my dimensions. Michael told me they usually kept stuff in specials sizes in the basement. I knew he was just calling the boys' department, but I didn't say anything. It would be a suit.

While we were waiting for that to come up, Michael took a long look at Ron. He went off and came back with a herringbone wool jacket, which fit the chest and shoulders but barely covered his elbows. Then Michael came with a huge one that almost covered the wrists but was big enough in the body for two Rons. They tried some more, and then Michael had to sit down. He was sweating lightly on his forehead.

"Look," he said. "I can get something specially made."

"They have stores for people my size," Ron said.

"Maybe you'd like a tie for now. Why don't you pick one out?"

"Yeah, Ron," I said trying to help. "No two ties the same."

So I got a suit and Ron got a tie. Michael showed him several ties, but Ron just shrugged his shoulders and took the nearest one, blue with gold squares. Michael offered a quick lesson in tie knotting, and Ron answered that he was too old for Boy Scouts. I wanted to wear my suit out of the store, like new shoes, so we waited for Michael to have it pressed. I gave him my old clothes, and he said he would bring them that night to dinner. I had a new suit. It was light blue, with wide lapels and white buttons that were probably carved from elephant tusks. We took the elevator downstairs. Everywhere I walked, I caught glimpses of myself in the mirrors an window reflections. I told Ron that the tie looked nice, but as soon as we were outside he yanked it from his neck and balled it into his pocket.

"What do you remember about our father?" Ron asked, when we were waiting for the bus.

I said I remembered what he looked like and that he sold insurance in a big building downtown. I said I remembered going to his office and looking down at all the little cars on the freeway. His secretary's name was Mary. But I didn't really remember any of these things. They were just things that Ron and Mom had told me over time.

"You know what I remember?" Ron said. "I remember his suits. They weren't cheap polyester like the one you're wearing. I used to camp out in his closet in the dark, wrapped up in his old army-issue sleeping bag, eating roasted peanuts. His suits used to hang down and tickle my ears. They were wool, and scratchy. They smelled like smoke. Then next morning Dad would find peanut shells in his shoes, and would come into my room, where I was sleeping, and wake me up by slapping the shoe against the wall, right over my head. In a couple days I would go back to his closet. I liked it in there."

"You did?"

"Sure," he said. "I made drawings on the walls that I never got in trouble for because nobody bothered to bend down and look. When Dad moved out and took his clothes, my drawings were revealed. I got away with it because so much else was going on."

"Wow." I tried to sound impressed.

"What do you mean, wow. Is that all you can say about a father leaving a family?" Ron didn't look at me as he talked.

"Why do you lead Mom on with Michael? Do you want her to get hurt again, is that what you want?"

"No."

"You make her think it's going to be all OK with him."

"Isn't it?"

"Man, sometimes you can be so stupid. What do you think we're getting these suits for?"

"Because they're on sale?"

"It's so we'll be men, and so we'll be able to take care of ourselves."

I didn't know what to do. I started to get cold, and I wished I hadn't given my parka and mittens to Michael. I was hoping that if I gave my face just the right look, one of the taxicabs would stop and give me a ride home for free. Several buses went by, they weren't ours. I turned my lapels up to cover my neck, even though I knew it looked stupid. It was a thin suit, a spring suit, fabric made from plastic, and I could feel the slight wind as if I weren't wearing anything. I wanted to stand close to Ron so he'd block the wind, but for every step I took toward him he took one away from me. Finally our bus came, and I got a seat next to a huge black lady. I tried to smile and make her like me, but my teeth were chattering and my breathing made me sound like I was growling at her.

Michael came that night just as Mom was setting dinner on the table, so they didn't get a chance to talk between themselves. Michael didn't say anything to Ron about the suit. Normally Michael liked to have a feast at the end of a hard week, and he liked to talk a lot. But now he was quieter. He kept his elbows off the table and set his glass down carefully and looked around at us only when he had his glass to his mouth like it was his first date with Mom all over again. Then Mom asked me to do the dishes, and she and Michael took the bottle of wine into her bedroom, which was on the same floor as the kitchen. They left the door open, and they were talking in hushed voices. I decided to have some ice cream, and I ended up eating the whole two quarts, right from the box, with a soup ladle. The ice cream made me really cold again, and I tried to wish warm air out of the heater vents. I expected Michael to spend the night—it was Saturday—but before too long he came out and closed the door behind him, walking straight through the living room and out the front door. After about fifteen minutes Mom came out with all her clothes on, the bottle empty at least a few days ahead of schedule. I was in the corner of the kitchen with only the stove lamp illuminating the room, and when Mom cracked the refrigerator the light caught me in the corner.

"What are you doing there, Louis? You're not spying on your mother, I hope."

"I was eating ice cream. I did the dishes."

"Why don't you have the lights on?" She closed the refrigerator, turned on a light, and then stuck a match and lit a cigarette. It'd been a while since I'd seen her smoke a cigarette—because she hadn't wanted us to start, she'd smoke only in her room when we weren't around, or in the store in the mornings—and I knew something was going on if she'd smoke one in front of me.

"I was saving electricity. I thought maybe we could turn on the heat if I turned out the lights for a while."

"Is that what you'd like, Louis, to turn the heat on? You can do it if you want. Go ahead. Fire it up. I wouldn't mind a sauna. I wouldn't mind a little warmth around here."

I wasn't going to do anything then, but she spun the dial on the thermostat, and I hear the old furnace boom in the basement and the blast of the pump igniting.

"There you go, Louis. That'll make everything all right for you now. You can be happy now."

"I didn't say it would do that, Mom."

"No, of course you didn't. Where are your friends Louis? It's Saturday night. Don't you have friends you should be out with?"

I didn't say anything then. I didn't bring friends home mostly because Ron would give me a hard time in front of them, and when you don't bring people to your house you don't get invited to theirs. I wanted to leave, but I also didn't, because I felt she needed me then, not in her usual way but in Ron's way—she needed me to be angry at.

Then Mom said, "Come over here, Louis." And I did that, I went and stood next to her, where she leaned up against the fridge. "Would it bother you if I opened another bottle? There's one in the cupboard over the sink, if you'd get it." So I did that, and I opened it, and I poured her some, but not much. It was red wine, and Ron had told me that was the strongest kind, and I didn't want her to have much more.

"What does Ron teach you, Louis? Does he teach you how to be nice to girls?"

"No."

"Your father used to say that he couldn't wait until you two got old enough and he could teach you about that." Then she reached out to me with her arms and pulled me to her body. I was almost as tall as she was, only a few inches shorter, and it was easy to hug her lightly. But when I started to pull away, the hug over, she said, "No, you'll never get a girlfriend that way. You have to hold them for a long time."

So we stood there in the kitchen, holding each other,

for several minutes. I was afraid to move, afraid to hug her any tighter or any softer. "When some man does come along to teach you about women, Louis, you remember this: you remember we like to be hugged. Don't let them skip over that part when they start talking about the other things."

"I wouldn't do that," I said. I could smell the smoke in her hair and on her clothes.

"You just stand here and hold. You don't try anything, you just make her feel good." Finally she let me go. "Why don't you see what your brother's doing upstairs?"

The next morning, Ron came in my room around nine-thirty and woke me up with a slap on the shoulder, saying I had to rake the lawn so he could burn the leaves. He threw a pair of jeans at my chest and said I'd slept through breakfast and had missed my chance to eat. I got a glass of milk then went outside. Ron had already started a fire in one of the garbage cans, which he had set down into he middle of the yard. He was burning the regular garbage, and it bled a deep black smoke that refused to rise to the sky.

The rake wasn't any help against leaves stiff with frost, so I had to use a pitchfork. I didn't know why we had to rake the leaves on that day, or in the winter at all, but it was either Mom's idea or Ron's, and I would surely lose an argument against either. Ron stood guard by the fire and shoveled my growing pile of leaves onto it. For a moment the fire would appear to go out — all that frost dripping onto the flames — and then the smoke would seep through again. In about twenty minutes I had done half the yard, and the neighborhood air was dark gray. The garbage can couldn't hold all the leaves, and burning them didn't seem to reduce their size, so he'd let the fire leap from the can into my pile. He shoveled some snow around it as a protective ring and told me not get too close, he was in charge. The neighbors started to call. First Judy Lightfoot from the house behind ours, and then Mr. Cable and Mr. Hawkes. What the hell were we burning? Who the hell was supervising it? Did we have a permit or should they call the cops? Mom took the calls, and it only made her mad at them. She stood by the door in her faded jeans and gray turtleneck and told us to keep going and make lots of smoke. Light the whole world on fire, she said. It started to snow lightly, but she didn't let it stop us. She waited until we were finished, and then she disappeared into her bedroom before I had a chance to talk to her.

For dinner that night Mom picked up little boxes of chicken and mashed potatoes. We ate and did not argue. Mom stared out the window at the falling sleet that kept the world hidden. Even our black ashes were hidden from sight under a sheet of ice. Ron finished quickly and did not ask to be excused when he left to watch television upstairs.

"It's Ron's birthday soon, isn't it?" Mom said.

I nodded. "A few weeks."

"What do you think he really wants?"

"He wants to go to Montana. He wants to drive there."

"Is that it, huh? It's that simple?" She let out a sigh.

I didn't know what she meant by that. I pulled one of Michael's magazines closer and started to flip through the pages.

"Well, maybe I should let him. He'd do a lot better hitch-hiking across the country than I would."

"It's cold there this time of year. People turn to ice statues just walking out to the car."

"Is that what he said?"

"And if you go out to feed the horses in the yard, sometimes it's snowing so hard that when you turn around you can't find your house."

She laughed a little. She started crumpling up our chicken boxes and napkins and threw them in the garbage. After she rinsed our glasses and put them away, she went back to the window.

Then she said, "We were close, you know. It was almost working."

"What, Mom?"

But she didn't answer. She went to the hallway closet, where she put on her yellow suit coat and scarf, which made her look like a schoolgirl at college. She came back into the kitchen only briefly.

"I can't stand this," she said.

"What, Mom?"

"I'm going to Michael's," she said. She opened the front door, and I could feel the draft. "I'll be back." Then she left.

So this is what I did: I sat at the kitchen table, reading the backs of cereal boxes and milk cartons, waiting for them to return. I waved my chicken bones over the candle flame until they were striped black zebra bones. I poured a glass of wine for myself, a real one, not just a shot glass, and I pulled out a stack of magazines to thumb through. I read old jokes over and over, but it was better than the milk cartons. I forced myself to laugh. Then I practiced laughing, because Michael had a laugh that boomed, and I wanted to have a laugh like that. It came from somewhere way in the back of his head, at the base of his skull, and it vibrated his nose as it came out.

Of course Ron came downstairs and wanted to know what was so funny. He had just taken a shower and his hair was combed in place. I said nothing was funny and that his hair looked nice. He asked where Mom was, as if I had kidnapped her, and I told him what had happened.

"She said she'd be back soon," I added.

Ron nodded. "What are you reading?"

"One of Michael's magazines. There's a fascinating article on the future of atomic energy."

"There is not."

"Sure there is." I had read the introduction in the table of contents, just the way I read the flaps on Mom's books. "Now they not only explode the atoms, they collapse them. The atoms implode."

"So?"

"They disappear. Poof! You've heard of black holes, this is how they start. They eat laboratories and buildings and earth. It's happening all over the East Coast." I hid my lies by offering him the magazine. "Here, read it yourself if you don't believe me."

"Nah." He opened the refrigerator, then closed it. He did the same with a couple of cabinets. "I made a basketball court in the television room," he said. "You want to see it?"

I followed him upstairs. He had pushed all the chairs and the couch up against the walls. A coffee can was nailed above the doorway, and a strip of masking tape marked the free-throw line a few feet away. A small Nerf ball sat in the middle.

Ron spotted me fifty points, and we agreed to a game to a hundred, which took about fifteen minutes. I failed to score a single point. It was impossible to get the ball in the can unless you stuffed it, which I could not quite manage. My balance was off from drinking the wine. Each time Ron drove past me and stuffed it, he also called a foul, which put him at the free-throw line. He couldn't make the shot either, but he could leap past me for the rebound. He had no need to dribble — he could cover the court in two steps — and sometimes he passed the ball to himself off the walls. Once, wrapped up in his defense, I tried his trick and accidentally threw the ball out the open window, where it soaked up a puddle like a sponge. Ron wrung it out and then dove past me for the last few buckets. Several times I expected him to get angry or dispute my calls, but he was all business, with a killer instinct that could not be stopped once begun. He gave no pointers, and throughout the game his only words were the increasing tally. At one hundred it was as if he woke from a trance sweaty and open-eyed, wondering what I was doing there.

Still Mom hadn't come home.

I sat down on the couch, and he turned on the television.

"Are you hungry?" I said.

"You already had dinner."

"But not a feast. I always feel like having a feast at the end of a hard week."

Ron kept flipping channels. "You haven't had a hard week," he said. "You're in sixth grade."

"Maybe we should call her," I said.

"Yeah, we probably should." Ron went for the phone book.

"What's his last name?" he asked.

I didn't know. He had always been Michael to me.

Not mister anybody. Not like the old boyfriends.

"Stupid," Ron said. He threw the book on the floor.

The book! I ran down to Mom's bedroom and looked at the book Michael had written, which she kept under her pillow. There was his last name, Asimakapoulos.

Ron got a busy signal.

"Michael probably got a call from his sister in Tacoma," I said.

We sat on the couch and didn't say anything for a while. Ron went into his room. I could hear the radio going. They were talking about cars. The wine had made me sleepy, and I curled up. I thought I would go to sleep like that, just like when Mom and Michael were around, but I couldn't get comfortable that way, so I went to bed. I stole some pillows from the sofa chair in the living room and put them on the foot of my bed, so from under the sheets it would feel like a dog was sleeping there.

When I woke, the snow had turned to rain, and the world was turning to mud. I ran downstairs to Mom's bedroom, but she wasn't there. I ran back upstairs and pushed Ron. He told me to go away and threw a pillow at me, but I wouldn't stop.

"They're not here," I said.

"Who?"

"Mom. Mom and Michael."

He got out of bed and turned off his radio. I could see his ribs under an oystery blue skin that hadn't seen sun in years. We sat on his bed. The gutters on our roof had flooded and the rain ran right down the window.

"Do you think we have to go to school today?" I asked.

"You can do what you want."

"It doesn't start for a couple more hours anyway. It'll probably start snowing again by then."

We sat there for some more time and just watched the rain. I wanted to know what time it was, but Ron didn't use an alarm clock. He believed he could condition himself to wake up at an exact time every day just by picturing the time in his mind before he went to sleep.

"They're probably stopping off at the pound," I said.

Then, a while later, I added, "And at the grocery. They're probably planning a big brunch for us. Smoked ham."

Ron pulled a blanket off my head and threw it over his shoulders. His hair was all bent up on one side. I took the other blanket and put it around my shoulders.

"And at the bakery," I said. "You know how Mom likes cinnamon rolls."

"Look, don't you get it? They're not coming back."

"What?"

"You see how happy they are with each other. They want to start a new life together. They want to have new kids of their own. They don't want to have anything to do with us."

"They don't?"

"They're probably halfway to California by now, cruising through the Siskiyou mountains in Michael's Impala."

"But Mom left all her stuff..."

"That's her old stuff. It's her old life. She's not taking that with her. Do you think Dad took anything with him when he left?" Ron spoke with scorn, not for my mother but for me, for not seeing this earlier.

"She said she'd be back."

"But she didn't say when."

"But, Ron, we're alone here."

"Shut up. You've got your suit, you can handle it."

I was numb. I was scared. Ron took me into the bathroom. We stood next to each other facing the mirror, the top of my head came even with his shoulder.

"What do you see?" he asked.

I saw myself. I saw his bent hair. I looked into our eyes for something else. I thought he was going to talk about how much older he was than me, how my face would thicken and an Adam's apple would grow in my throat and how my wavy hair would begin to curl. I expected a sermon about how I was going to have to grow up fast. How I'd have to become more like him.

"Now step on the toilet," he said. The toilet was right beside me, its rim had been pushing up to my shin. When I stood, my shoulder came even with Ron's, our eyes on equal level. "What do you see now?" he asked.

I turned to the mirror. But now my head was above the mirror, I could only see my mouth and neck and trunk extending down to my feet on the led of the toilet.

"This is how I live," he said. "I have to bend down to see myself."

I could only see his mouth as he talked. I couldn't see his eyes, I didn't know where they were looking, but I imagined they stared off to the upper right, as if he were talking to someone else.

"I have one for you," he said. "This one's going to kill you for sure."

"No," I said. "It's impossible to kill me." He was finally

getting to me, all his meanness.

"I break both your ankles with a spike mace, and you've lost three quarts of blood. Then I tie you in ropes and throw you into a pool of starving great white sharks."

"Great whites hate the taste of rope," I said.

"Not when they haven't eaten in two weeks. Not when they're starving."

"I quickly swim to the bottom and pull the plug on the pool. The water runs out and the sharks are left yapping like harmless poodles."

"You're still bleeding."

"But I'm still alive," I said.

"Yes," he said. "You're still alive."

Ron ran out of the room and went into his, where he started packing a duffel bag with his clothes. He picked out his jeans and his rugby and flannel shirts and rolled them into tight balls.

"What are you doing?" I said.

"I'll be sixteen in two weeks anyway," he said. "I might as well get a head start."

The bag quickly filled. He unplugged his radio and put that in there, along with a toothbrush and a towel. He went down to the kitchen and got a small knife and a can opener and three cans of beans. He didn't even have to think; he was just checking off a mental list that he must have gone over many times.

"I was going to wait 'til summer," he said. He zipped up the bag and set it outside his door. "Look," he said. "I could give it a week. We've got some food downstairs to live on, and that would give you a couple of days to get your own bag and make some plans. I was going to take the umbrella, but you can have it."

I didn't know what to do. I thought I could handle this but I just couldn't, not with Ron around. I decided to go back to bed, to crawl under the covers and kick the pillows onto the floor. I didn't want to believe him, but I found myself making plans. I still had the house, and I could just live here on my own, go to school during the day. I could get a job in the afternoons bagging groceries and steal some food from the storeroom. I wouldn't even have to tell anyone that my mom was gone. The milkman brought a half gallon of low-fat and some cottage cheese on Tuesdays. I could eat cottage cheese if I had some jam. Then I remembered we had most of last summer's raspberry jam in the freezer. It would be OK. It would be tough on my birthday and on holidays, but people lived alone all the time.

We'd come so close — Michael'd been there, in our lives. It was almost working. I drew my legs up to my chest and closed my eyes and counted to ten, then I went over my plan again. People lived alone all the time.

I heard a car outside, its doors opening and closing. I threw off the covers and ran to the window as I heard voices, two voices. Michael's Impala sat at the curb. In one arm Michael held an umbrella over Mom's head. Draped over the other arm, protected by a thin layer of plastic, was a brown herringbone suit.

With my arms high over my head, I ran, first in tight circles, then out my door and into Ron's room, victory on my lips. But he was not in his room. I could see him through his window — he was out back again, jumping, lead sacks on his bony ankles. He jumped from a puddle and landed in his own footsteps, taking off again before the water could cover his shoes. His pants, shirt, and hair clung to his body. Near the tops of his jumps his face clenched.

With the sleeve of my pajama top I wiped away the mist on the window. From his bed I stole a green wool surplus blanket and draped it over my shoulders, and I watched my brother and said nothing, even as I heard the front door open and the voices come closer, calling our names: "Lou? Ron? Louis?" In ten minutes I'd be downstairs, trying not to crack the yolks on the eggs Mom had bought as Michael checked the length of Ron's new trousers. But at that moment I had lost my thoughts—I counted up toward fifty, waiting for his set to end.

Ten-year-old **Jasmine Sun** *describes herself as curious, sometimes stubborn, and a daydreamer. She likes to spend her time reading on the big comfy couch in her family's living room. Her favorite place in the Pacific Northwest is Deer Lake on Whidbey Island, where she and her family vacationed once. They caught crabs and clams and had a wonderful seafood dinner every night. Jasmine plans to become a fiction writer or a nature photographer.*

THE MYSTERY IN THE MANSION

by Jasmine Sun

CYNTHIA WAS DEVASTATED. Her family was moving to Washington, and for all she knew it was a rainy, dull, gray-skies sort of place. Oh, how she wanted to stay in Florida, with the palms swaying in the breeze and the sunny beaches. Cynthia currently lived in Orlando, in the heart of all the action. Yes, the big-city feeling sometimes could get slightly overwhelming, but it had to be better than some wet, unexciting city across the country, right? Cynthia's parents didn't even consider the fact that the location was unacceptable! Plus —

"Cynthia! Get over here! The taxi's waiting! Do you want to miss it?" hollered her mom.

Yes, I do want to miss the taxi, Cynthia thought. Then we can stay here forever. But it was no use; her parents would find a way. She dragged her suitcase over to the door and said goodbye to her home.

"CYNTHIA!"

Never mind. She hopped into the taxi with the peeling paint and shut the door. She stared out the window, and eventually everything became a blur and she fell asleep. When Cynthia finally woke up, the land was different. It was more green and hilly, but still quite dreary and dull.

"Where are we?" she asked.

"Almost there; we're in Tacoma, nearing Seattle." Her dad answered. Cynthia started staring at the window again, and it was raining. Too much rain, she thought, even though she hadn't been there before.

"Guess what, Cynthia?" asked Cynthia's mom. "We get to meet Uncle Bill! Isn't it exciting?"

"Who the heck even is Uncle Bill? And no, it's not exciting," groaned Cynthia. Her mom and dad sighed, with weary and somewhat tired looks on their faces.

"I forgot, we never told her who my little bro Bill is!" muttered Cynthia's dad to her mom.

"Oh, Cynthia doesn't know what she's in for," her mom said.

After a long while, the car screeched to a stop in front of some large iron gates. Beyond, a huge lush green lawn greeted the family and Cynthia's parents were enchanted by the beautiful music of the salmon creek. Even Cynthia was astounded at this grand place. Better yet, a humongous mansion stood behind the magnificent front yard, as big as a castle.

"Hey, Cynthia, do you still miss Florida?" asked Cynthia's dad.

"A little, but not as much as before. Are we going to live here? This looks like Bill Gates's house or something!" shouted Cynthia.

"Do you know why? That's because it is! My little

brother is one of the richest men in America. We never told you, well, mostly to keep you from going hyper. Plus, just because your uncle's a billionaire doesn't mean that you can turn into a spoiled brat."

Cynthia was speechless. Sure, she was a little annoyed at her parents for not telling her earlier, but mostly Cynthia was in awe of the place she was going to live in for a whole week!

Finally, the big gates opened, and the little red car looked miniscule next to the enormous mansion and the driveway that it drove on. A jovial-looking man opened the front door, and welcomed the family in.

"Just park right there, and come in! So nice to see you, Mark, and look there at your beautiful wife! Pleasure to meet you, Amy. Oh, and you must be Cynthia! You'll love it here, I'm sure of it." Uncle Bill sure seemed to be a nice man, not to mention a billionaire! Cynthia shared a firm but warm handshake with Uncle Bill, and then she hopped right on into the grand hallway.

Uncle Bill handed each member of the family a little microchip so the music and other preferences would change from one room to the next depending on what each person wanted. For Cynthia, it was like taking a trip to the future.

First, Uncle Bill showed everyone to their rooms, and each person got a gigantic bedroom and a king-sized bed. Cynthia was absolutely positive that living in Seattle, well, Medina to be exact, would be amazing. And even when Cynthia would have to move back to the other, much smaller mansion, it couldn't be bad, with *the* Bill Gates living nearby!

Everyone slept soundly, except for Cynthia. She was awake peering out the window at the stunning view of Lake Washington, watching the sunset. Suddenly, she heard the phone ring. It was ten o'clock. Who would be calling this late? Somebody on the floor reserved for Uncle Bill answered, and since only Bill Gates was allowed on that floor it had to be Uncle Bill! Why wasn't anybody allowed on that floor? Maybe it was where Bill developed one-of-a-kind ideas for new software, and he didn't want anyone to see. But that seemed unlikely, as when traveling past level four in the glass elevator it seemed to be just normal rooms, just fancier and decked with famous works of art.

Cynthia finally decided that it was none of her business what Bill Gates did in secret. It was probably just to get some privacy from flashing cameras and newspaper reporters and such. However, Cynthia once again became curious when she heard Uncle Bill on the phone, ever so faintly.

"Yes, they're still locked up. Everything's fine, don't worry about my guests, they're my relatives!" said Uncle Bill. Cynthia was confused as to why someone would be locked up, but then she assured herself that it was probably a something, not someone. But just in case, Cynthia wanted to listen some more. It was half past ten though, and she finally drifted away to sleep.

The next morning when Cynthia woke up at her usual time of seven-thirty, she whiffed the mouth-watering aroma of bacon and eggs. Yum, Cynthia thought. She put on her new fuzzy flannel robe and hurried downstairs to the first floor for breakfast. She noticed that the floors were heated, so her feet didn't freeze so early in the morning. This was the life!

Cynthia seemed to have forgotten about the previous night, as she was really living it up at the Gates' mansion.

Since Uncle Bill had so much money, nobody stopped her from doing all the things she wanted to learn back in Florida, which she didn't even miss anymore! Each day her schedule was perfect. Not too busy, but not like there wasn't anything to do for half the day. Even if Cynthia did have spare time on her hands, she could always go to the indoor pool or play tennis in the ginormous backyard.

Her agenda went like this: Get up at seven-thirty each morning, and ask a personal chef to prepare breakfast. Do something until nine-thirty, when she would would go swimming in the lake. Have kayaking lessons at ten, and lunch at noon. At one o'clock, take trip to somewhere like the mall, a beach, a hike in the mountains, or something else until six-thirty for dinner. After dinner, watch a movie, or read. Go to bed at ten.

One night, Cynthia was taking the elevator up to the fifth floor to look at the stars through a telescope on the stargazing deck. When she passed the fourth floor, Cynthia thought she heard a muffled scream coming from a painting on the forbidden level. She saw Uncle Bill walk up to the work of art and thump it, and then walk away. Cynthia would have watched some more, but in a matter of seconds the elevator had carried her up to the stargazing deck.

Usually, Cynthia saw nothing but stars while looking up into the dark sky, but today was different. She was thinking about what she saw in the elevator. It was weird. Cynthia felt she had to investigate, even though she was pretty sure it was just her mind playing tricks on her. One of Cynthia's favorite books was *Harriet the Spy*, and ever since she read it in the third grade she had wanted to be a detective.

The next day, Cynthia got her chance to do some

spying. Uncle Bill had gone out for the day for an important business meeting of some sort and her mom and dad were meeting with some other long-lost relatives, so Cynthia had the house to herself. But once she got inside the elevator, Cynthia realized that there was no fourth floor button! There had to be some way of getting up, so there was probably a secret elevator.

Detective Cynthia searched every closet for a secret elevator, until she found that in the storage space on floor two there was a spiral staircase up to the fourth floor. Cynthia immediately found her way to the Jackson Pollock painting, and lifted it up. There was a locked door, and that's when Cynthia knew that she had discovered something great. Cynthia peered out the window with the special binoculars she had brought along, and realized that Uncle Bill was coming back on I-90. There wasn't much time.

The question of how to open the lock at first stumped Cynthia. Then, she remembered from a book she had read about spying that you could pick a lock with a bobby pin. Cynthia took one out of her bun, and wiggled it around in the lock until finally, she heard a satisfying click. Uncle Bill was rounding the corner, observed Cynthia.

Opening the door, she was shocked to find what was inside. There were Bill and Melinda Gates, tied up with a sock in each of their mouths! They also seemed to be astonished. So "Uncle Bill" really wasn't the real Bill Gates, and he was an imposter who kidnapped the real ones? It was a lot to take in. But Cynthia quickly took out her Swiss Army knife and cut through the ropes and took the socks out of their mouths.

"What the heck?" gasped Bill Gates. He looked

around. "Thanks," he said.

"Go back inside," said Cynthia. "When my uncle gets home, I'll say 'look what I found' and show him you guys. But first, I will have called 9-1-1. Got it?" Bill and his wife nodded.

"That man's your uncle?" asked Melinda with a touch of disbelief in her voice. Instead of answering, Cynthia put her finger to her lips, and hurried the frightened couple back behind the painting. Cynthia went back to her room, and looked out. Police cars were a block ahead of "Uncle Bill," and they rang the doorbell just in time.

When they entered, Cynthia explained the whole situation to them. "Uncle Bill" came in just as Cynthia finished their story, and the police put handcuffs on him right away. Cynthia looked smug, while her uncle seemed almost angry.

"Hey, Uncle Bill, look what I found!" exclaimed Cynthia, and led the police team along with her uncle up the secret stairs and showed them the door behind the painting. Bill and Melinda hopped right out, and thanked her.

"Oh, my gosh, I just realized that Uncle Bill didn't find a wife to pretend to be Melinda!" cried Cynthia. "It should have been so obvious!"

"Don't worry, kid. You did just fine," said the chief of police. Cynthia smiled.

EPILOGUE

In the end, everything was fine. Cynthia's uncle went to jail, and the real Bill Gates offered to fly Cynthia back to Florida whenever she liked, but Cynthia declined, instead wanting a CityPass for each member of the family.

Lyall Bush *is the executive director of Northwest Film Forum and was the creator of the Hugo Literary Series at the Richard Hugo House, where he was previously the executive director. He has been published in* The Stranger *and the* Iowa Review *among others. Bush loves to read the poems of Jorie Graham and the essays of Ralph Waldo Emerson or watch beautiful Chinese films on rainy afternoons.* "The Curse of the Golden Flower, *for example: amazing."*

POP SONG

by Lyall Bush

THE DARK NIGHT, the light coming up to the house, the transitions from point A to point B, the smells of the sea and the forest floor, the shadows on the road in, the scent of trees and leaves, the number of people there and what they wore, the movements of hands in the not-large rooms. All of it happened, though not all like I will tell it. Most would be no more possible to change than it would be to alter the drifting of snow in the night. The motives of the two guys, what happened in the house while I was on the beach, the strange music, the incomprehensible talk in the kitchen. It's like desert gods: figures appear in tent flaps, and you read, "and they stood there." And then something new begins. Nobody understands why, or what it means, or even if they are gods. Only that they appeared and then things were different.

I heard parts of this from Jason, who I will call Jaime here, and from Jon, who I call Todd, who seemed to know things no one else did. Other names are also changed: Lana, the flight attendant, is Sylvia, and the guy with the hippie face is Luke, not Timothy or—I forget—Anthony? The fight was, in a way, more dramatic, more visceral than the way I describe it, because most of what happened, the pushing and shouting, was a way for two men to say what was going on inside them. So much of it seemed to have to do with people turning their heads to see the flesh of fists in sudden combination, the emotional yelling. While he was defending himself, Luke said, for example, "I'm *honorable*, for Chrissake." What did that mean?

So that was it: a party at the turn of the year, the smell of beach air, pre-party swimming, alcohol, Brazilian something, Air Supply, the midnight swinging of fists, a woman with a way of moving in rooms and cars, as Jaime said, that made men lose their train of thought. And shouting about love.

My name is Rich. It's not my real one, but my real one is not so far from it that you couldn't guess. I am like the guy I portray myself to be. I teach at a small college in Seattle. I wear sweaters with holes in them and comfortable shoes. At parties I eat potato chips out of my hand and talk as if my nervous system had been compromised by the time I had spent as a war correspondent for the Victorian novel. I tell twenty-year-olds that the subterranean romantic alliances in *The Mill on the Floss* have stakes that encompass all England, for example. In my spare time I get together with friends and watch Taiwanese films about blowing curtains. I am sometimes something of a jerk; I have shut down regular dinner table conversation by saying that there was no Althusserian lacunae in the way the lamb was done but it did speak to the political unconscious that the mashed potatoes were appropriately rustic.

But the story starts with the other guys, who I heard

about from Todd. They were on the viaduct, in shining rain, at night, driving to the West Seattle ferry, listening to the Flaming Lips. Clayton, who was behind the wheel, cranked the music, and as he sang his long blond hair moved like a thin shirt on the line. You probably know the songs. When they came to the one that speculated about how things may have gotten too heavy for Superman, Robbie, who was in the passenger seat, yanked on the hand-strap as if he were struggling to free himself from his captors, making grunting, teeth-baring ape sounds from *2001: A Space Odyssey*: "arngh, arngh, arngh, arngh!" The events of the day had unleashed something in them, and Clayton in particular let the songs on the tape, up to that point, go through him. The thought of something shining all around made Robbie take on the other available role: angry, vaguely simian harmonizer.

The music wasn't their usual choice, but it gave them a strange kind of energy and dulled the sting of the bulls-eye tattoos they had just gotten, which in turn made it easier to anticipate meeting Sylvia, who had invited them to the New Year's Eve party at a beach house on Vashon. They had met her in the coffee line on the Hill after a barista slipped on some spilled soy and the orders of shorts with room and double talls paused long enough for her to hear Robbie telling Clayton about a friend of theirs whose videotape of his tricks at the Ballard skate bowl had been embedded in a skateboard blog and then gotten forwarded so much that now a company called You/Who was flowing decks to him. Sylvia turned at that point, lifted her face up to them, and asked them if they had ever visited the original Jeff Ho skateboard shop in Santa Monica, and before they could answer added that this line was a far cry from the friendly skies. She had come from Sydney a day ago and had either lost or gained a day, she wasn't even sure. She just needed coffee. She was tired but pretty, as Todd later said.

They told her more about their friend and that he could do moves they were still working on, like the ollie pop, the indy 720, the loop of death, the caveman, the nosebone. They demoed a couple for her, their shoulders and arms in motion. The line started to move again. Clayton added that he was working on a salad shooter. Sylvia said come on; he was making that up to test her. He said no, he wasn't, why would he lie. Robbie said he was working up to working on that one.

Sylvia turned around to order, and after she had paid said, "Do either of you fly much? At night? " Her voice went dreamy when she said it.

Neither flew very much.

"Most people fly during the day. But at night it's dreamier."

It was the end of the year and the days felt like small, dim squares on the calendar. Sylvia's idea, her image, of flying sparked in both guys an idea about the future. Their morning and afternoon had been the opposite of that: gray drizzle and mist until the windows, railings, curbs, and cars all shone as if lightly oiled. It was December, the dark transit of the year, and days had already settled in to this. From the window of the copy center, at Park and Boylston, they could watch people move past in a maze-y shuffle, carrying coffee cups and rip-able bags of take-out as if they had just left the emergency room.

Clayton and Robbie, differently blond, had anxiety about copying and duplicating. They didn't trust that copies would be actual duplicates. Both were certain each copy was less real than the last and they became friends when they were first stoned at work and talked about it. They looked a little alike, too, and eventually they became room-mates. And on this day they told Melissa, their boss, that they had gotten a call about a leak in their apartment, and after lunch, with the rain letting up a little, they left and headed to a matinee of the director's cut of *Donnie Darko* at the Egyptian. They emerged at four, in a jittery funk about falling jets, wormholes, and the end of the world. They crossed the street, and up another block, and by agreement took the five steps down into a brightly-lit half-basement with five tables and a couple of heavy guys behind the counter. They flipped through books of images, made decisions, got the bulls-eye tattoos around their navels and then, their bodies on fire, they left, had burritos, and walked into the coffee place where Sylvia turned and tipped her face. They were in their late twenties, young enough to have a sense that there was something they ought to be driving toward, but not old enough to know what missing it could mean.

I was late, myself. Off the ferry I had gotten stuck behind a slow-moving timber truck that was hauling freshly cut trees with scabby bark still on and signs on the rear that had, on either side, read, "Passing side" (an arrow pointing left) and "Suicide" (one pointing right). I took a right and descended immediately down a road that instantly littered the wind-shield with pine twigs. When the road stopped I parked and walked to a scruffy beach and stopped to listen to the soft inlet water. Nearby was a glinting orange sign that read

DANGER CABLE CROSSING in large letters.

I drove back to the main road and this time took a right, and immediately shadows began to pass over the windshield. Heavy, wild berry bushes and weeds on either side became bigger trees, and I rolled down my window and felt the ocean air before I saw another beach and a large, rundown house. I parked on the grass between two cedar trees, and felt good getting to the party an hour and a half before the New Year. Two blond-haired guys were getting out of another car at the same time and we talked and introduced ourselves. It was Robbie and Clayton, of course, who were the same height, short-legged, and had slightly marsupial eyes. As we walked to the house Robbie kept up a conversation about the heaviness of the water that they had evidently been having since they got on the ferry. They seemed to be imagining skateboarding over it.

Then Sylvia, not Jaime, was at the door to welcome us. She was wearing a coat and grabbed the two guys especially and led us in to the living room where a couple of dozen people were drinking and listening to two guys playing songs on acoustic guitar. I'd met her a month before with Jaime, who told me they were "sort of" seeing each other. Now, by way of introduction, she told us there was a double party, one in the main house and another in her place, which was upstairs and in a separate apartment. I was absorbing this when the back door opened with a creak of aluminum and Jaime padded in, barefoot, his hair soaking. He was smiling a weary philosopher smile I recognized from other events at the college.

"Swimming," he said, not stopping. "See you in a minute." Todd tapped my shoulder and I turned twice be-

826 SEATTLE

236

WHAT TO READ IN THE RAIN · 2011

fore I found him. He was smiling, with a Brian Wilson dot in his eyes. We shook hands, his crushing mine while the band started a soft, acoustic version of "Kashmir." I saw Sylvia lead Robbie and Clayton into another room. In profile, she looked like a Renaissance portrait.

Then Jaime was beside me, his hair pushed back, motioning me to come with him into the kitchen. The other half of the party was there, and a few people in sleeveless fleece jackets were talking about a retreat they had just come back from. Jaime looked at me while they talked about electrics, magnetism, carbon. Robbie and Clayton were there, too, and someone near them said that what was "amazing" about the retreat was learning that the only difference between "us and stars is time." Todd was suddenly near me again and he giggled.

The kitchen was large, with an old, car-green refrigerator, dirty butcher-block counters, and lamps with comically small shades. While people kept talking Sylvia turned to the sink to show the two boys how she mixed rum and cokes with mint leaves for people who, on cue, began to arrive to pick them up. For a minute the whole party was in the kitchen and the kitchen was full of odd smiles, little eyes, and hands reaching for glasses. Robbie and Clayton fetched glasses and ice and did quick finger-stirs that made Sylvia tip her head back and laugh.

I turned to Todd. "Did someone just say 'dreammouth'?"

Todd's eyes widened and he took me in for five beats. "Gem rod," he said, pointing to his spine.

"I unfortunately have back trouble," I said.

Todd stared at me. "Your spine isn't your back," he said and laughed. He pointed to a guy with a beard and said,

"Yes, he's here."

"Who?"

"It's Luke," he said, pointing again. "He's Jesus."

I remembered him. Jaime introduced me to Luke a year before, at the last New Year's party, as a friend who had just come back from a dig in North Africa. He had taken up field recordings. Another song started, and it seemed that the words were about Mark or Luke.

"I'll shout it out, who killed the Kennedys?" the singer whispered brightly.

"One of these days we'll get you there," Todd said, his mouth close to my ear.

"What is it called again?"

"None of your effing business," he said, and laughed. "How are you, man? What are you reading these days?"

"Everything," I said.

Clayton came up. "The band is weird," he said, and snickered. He took a drink from a bottle and moved his hair.

Todd said, "It's 'Sympathy for the Devil,' man."

"Sympathy for what?" Clayton said.

"What is 'everything'?" Todd asked.

"I don't know," I said to Clayton. And to Todd: "I don't know if I can afford it." Then I turned to Clayton and stuck out my hand.

"I'm Rich," I said.

"I know. We met outside."

"Oh yeah." I smiled, but I'd offended him.

"Sylvia says you're smart and all. Are you like a knowledge worker?" He looked down, snickering a little. A couple wedged between us, headed back in for more drinks.

"I'm an assistant professor at the U," I said. "So I

guess I am. I'm credentialed."

"My friend is credentialed up the yin yang," Todd said.

"I guess that takes a lot of money," Clayton said. "To do that and all."

Then Robbie was there. He looked at Clayton. "OK, time to show people the tats?" Each picked up his shirt to show us the sore-looking marks circling their navels.

"Wow," was all I could say. "Is this a code? Are you guys archers?"

The fight wiped away a lot of what else happened. The guys on guitar started a slow version of "Around and Around," and I went to listen to them before going back to the kitchen, where Todd was talking to Robbie and Clayton about the history of ink. Other things happened after that. Midnight crept up, people left even before the countdown, I heard, to dance to power ballads from Air Supply and Steve Perry at the "other" party, other people clumped at the back door smoking and talking about mantles and cores, and what next year was going to bring. I heard Todd saying he knew certain things just based on surfing. Things broke: someone danced into a lamp and smashed a light bulb. Someone else dropped a glass. I moved and accidentally kicked a bottle into Clayton's ankle. Jaime, who had somehow gotten drunk on rum and cherry Coke, bent to sweep up the broken glass with a shaving brush and he slipped on the wet floor. "Help me, man," he said, which made Luke say, "I don't know if anyone can help you, Jaime. You're drunk and bleeding." He was trying to be funny. He hoisted his glass and said "Happy New Year, man." But he didn't help Jaime up.

That was the preamble to the fight. The broken glass, Sylvia moving around everyone like a thread, the seawater smell filtering in with the scent of pinecones and pine needles. The fight started after midnight, after the toasting, after the band started into an impromptu "Jungle Boogie"/Jimi Hendrix sequence. Before that I stepped out the back door and found Sylvia, sloshed and holding a champagne bottle. We talked for a minute through and across the smokers until she said, holding a champagne bottle, something about being "attrasha" and then "la la," or sounds like that. When I went towards her to hear the rest she pushed me away, the grit of sand that had blown onto the patio making her a little unsteady. I said I was going for a walk and after a beat she said, "Just a sec," and kicked off her shoes and ducked past me inside the house. In the porch light she turned, her face circled by the fur. A minute later she hadn't come back so I walked down the stairs to the water alone, following dark, patchy grass past a portable grill to concrete steps that led down to sand and seaweed and the beach. I heard water moving before I saw it, black and slow and white-edged, lapping softly. The sky was black plaited straw.

Clayton was there, throwing twigs and other debris into the tide. He looked around when I came up. "Yo," he said, almost silently, as he moved as if to give me room.

"Something's going on up there," he said.

"Everybody's drunk and the band is probably playing Burt Bacharach now," I said.

"No, man—people are weird. They are talking about God." His face was smiling but he was checking my reaction.

"It's New Year's eve," I said. "No one knows what to do." I didn't know what to say. He was kind of right.

"Things used to be a lot cooler here." He was holding another twig to throw.

"Once we were depressive gardeners," I said. "Now we are quietly raging gardeners." I picked up some stones for myself. "What's with the tattoo, if you don't mind me asking?"

"Circle," he said, looking down. He seemed about to say something else and then he stopped.

"If it's around your belly button it's kind of a funnel."

"Hey, that's good," he said. He looked down. "Funnel."

The water lapped away from us. Somewhere nearby a random string of caps went off with lots of teakettle whistling.

We walked back and slid open the screen door and right then the fight was starting. Robbie and Luke were pulling at each other's clothes, their faces hot and distorted. Sylvia was off to the side, her collar down. Luke had an earnest bearded expression, and just behind him Jaime stood looking moon-faced, frightened and balding. Then his shirt was off and he was grappling with the other two, pulling off Robbie's long-sleeved waffle undershirt and exposing a sunken chest and a slightly pregnant lower belly. The fight was about who had lied about another broken bottle, pieces of which still lay on the floor, reflecting glinting bits of flesh and teeth. Then Jaime was in it, suddenly breathing hard, and Luke was saying to him, or to Robbie, in a dream-yelling voice, "Just tell me. Just tell me. Just tell me!" Luke waved his Jesus hair out of the way. He pushed Robbie away easily but with some panic. Then Sylvia was behind Luke, her silver hair flashing in the glass and along the old refrigerator chrome, and I wondered how it had really started. Something radiated from her. The men in the group were setting down their bottles, the women calling out the names of each man.

The guitar playing had stopped. Robbie and Luke slipped on something and they were down, Jaime with them. Each was making noises in his throat. I looked over and Todd was grinning and Sylvia was touching her collar. In the loose circle around the fight everyone looked beautiful and bright. I looked at the bare chests and the beer bellies of the guys wrestling. Around the room everyone shone a little.

That was ten years ago and it doesn't make any more sense now. The fight was suddenly over—some of us pulled the three guys off each other and held them for a couple of minutes while they lunged and they stopped breathing so hard and tried to figure out how to walk away with a little dignity. Someone swept the glass onto a piece of cardboard (more light and flesh moving over the broken surfaces) and then, when it seemed to be over, Luke, who hadn't spoken much all night, said, as if to get another fight going, "Why don't you love me, Jaime?" It wasn't that kind of revelation, but I put it together in my mind with what people were saying about magnetism and silicon and spines, and the retreat so many of them had been on. But what did Luke mean? Was there something about the uselessness of the occasion, the nearness of nature, that made him say it? I went back to my car, brushed the twigs off the windshield, and drove to the ferry, and for days, back in the city, before Todd filled me in and reminded me about the copy center and Robbie and Clayton, all I could think of was the fight I saw, it seemed, first in the broken glass, Luke crying out, the scrubby beach, the silhouettes of trees that all looked alike, all around us, all looking out at the same thing.

Eli Sanders *always carries a list of karaoke songs in his pocket. You know, just in case. He is an associate editor for Seattle's weekly newspaper* The Stranger, *for which he has written numerous profiles, Seattle stories, and articles on sex and gay issues. When the Seattle skies turn gray, he likes to read recipes for soup or sit in eucalyptus-infused steam baths. His favorite place to go when it rains?* "The Volunteer Park Conservatory— best radiators in the city."

THE JEWISH PROBLEM: MY FAMILY, MY CITY, MY RELIGION

FROM *The Stranger, December 19, 2006*

by Eli Sanders

1. BLOOD, 1977

IN A LARGE HOUSE on the edge of Seattle's Central District, a Jewish family gathers in their dining room, overlooking the wooded ravines of Frink Park. Two generations are on hand to celebrate the arrival of a third, and a mohel has been summoned, an old, dumpy man carrying a little black case.

Inside the case are the instruments he will use to execute the circumcision in accordance with Old Testament instructions. The baby, eight days old as suggested by the Book of Genesis, is sucking on a cloth soaked in red wine. He appears quite happy. In the distance, out the windows, through the trees, is Lake Washington, and beyond the lake, the Cascade Mountains. It is, historically speaking, a surprisingly wet and leafy place to find Jews conducting an ancient desert ritual.

The older generation of the family includes a man named Moses, now going by Martin, and his wife Franzi, now going by Frances, both of them Americanized refugees who fled Vienna, with some difficulty, after Hitler annexed Austria in 1938. Martin has jettisoned his Austrian accent and joined American medical circles. Frances is less excited about linguistic assimilation, and speaks with a flagrant disregard for English grammar. Their son is a refugee of a different sort, having fled the East Coast for Seattle. He is the new father.

On the new mother's side, the elders include William, born in Brooklyn, in 1915, to two Jewish refugees from Russia: Heiman Massarsky, who came to this country to escape Russian anti-Semitism and conscription into the Czar's army, and Rose Dubroflonski, who followed him. With William is his wife Eva, now going by Eve, also the child of Russian immigrants. Earlier in his life, William managed to get into the Ivy League, a trick at a time when elite schools were trying to limit their numbers of Jewish students. Earlier in her life, Eve worked for the Red Cross in the Pacific theater during World War II. They met in Okinawa, where William was serving as a military translator, and were married after the war.

This gathering is hardly the first Jewish circumcision ceremony to be performed in the damp outpost of Washington state, where the first Jew is believed to have arrived as early as 1845, back when the state was still a territory. But the gathering is typical of Washington Jewry in the complicated genealogical paths that lead up to it, in the unorthodox mix of participants who have assembled, and in the wildly divergent brands of faith among them. A relative on the edge of the crowd will be heard muttering after the ceremony about it having been "barbaric." The parents, no fans of strict religiosity themselves, are nevertheless having the ceremony and will soon enroll their child in Jewish daycare (though it will be a daycare run by Kadima, a leftist Jewish group). The elder men are pleased, sipping wine and wearing yarmulkes.

Holding the baby is another member of the older generation, Nora, a communist atheist Jew from Canada, who sees no contradiction in any of those terms. She is related to the baby by her marriage to a man whose own connection to the child traces back through Vancouver, B.C., to Pennsylvania, British Palestine, and, ultimately, Vienna. Nora is fulfilling the role of the sandek, sometimes translated as "godparent," the person who holds the baby while the mohel creates the biblically-commanded "covenant of the flesh."

The baby, in other words, has a godmother who does not believe in God. Which raises the question, never far from any American Jewish gathering, particularly in a relatively un-Jewish place such as this: What exactly is being celebrated? The continuation of a culture? A binding genetic affiliation? A respect for shared tradition? A religion?

There is no time to address all of that. The mohel is ready. The baby screams. Blood watches blood.

The baby, I should mention, is me.

2. MOUNTAINS, 1917

One of the problems of Washington Jews is that they have been, and remain, very much out of context. The Jew of the modern imagination is a big-city dweller—a persecuted minority in the capitals of Europe, a resident of bursting tenements in early 20th-century America, the urbane sophisticate of contemporary Manhattan. By contrast, in the boxes of worn photos housed at the University of Washington's Jewish Archives, the Jews of this state pose with evergreen trees as backdrops, wearing Stetsons and dirty work boots, selling equipment to gold prospectors.

Washington Jews have been, and remain, Jews in the wilderness, though a far more evergreen kind of wilderness than the one talked about in the Book of Exodus. In the 2003 book *Family of Strangers*, one of the few serious works of history about the Jews of this state, there is a black-and-white image of fourteen Jews, two of them from one of Seattle's most prominent Jewish families, the Alhadeffs, standing in a mountain pass, snow-capped peaks in the background, big, outdoorsy smiles on all of their faces.

It is a striking photo because over some 4,000 years of Jewish history, snowy mountaintops have never played much of a role in Jewish iconography. Practically every other geologic form has made an appearance: parting seas, deserts in which a tribe could get lost for forty years, farmland, rivers, marshland, the hills of Jerusalem, the flatlands and forests of Eastern Europe, the harbors of New York. As far as big Jewish mountains go, however, there is really only one, and it is not a mountain in the Pacific Northwest sense. It is Mt. Sinai, where the heavens are purported to have erupted as Moses climbed to the top to receive two stone tablets inscribed by God.

I have been to that mountaintop. There was no snow. There weren't even any trees. It is a low mountain in the barren midsection of the Sinai Peninsula, a triangle of land between mainland Egypt and Israel, a cracked moonscape the color of sun-baked mud. When I climbed Mt. Sinai in the summer of 1997, to absolutely no revelation whatsoever, I slept at the top, needed only a light sleeping bag to keep warm, and felt very distant from the mountaintops on which I hiked and camped as a younger man. The summit of Mt. Sinai is about 7,500 feet, roughly half the height of Mt. Rainier, where, on a lower flank of that mountain, I once slept, shivering, in an igloo I'd built with members of my Boy Scout troop—none of them Jewish.

The modern imagination is not, of course, correct in its casting of Jews as exclusively urban creatures. But the focus of this imagination on the urban Jew is understandable, a product of the places that Jews were pushed to, and through, over the course of a history that is in large part the story of exile and expulsion. Jews have been kicked out of ancient Israel and fifteenth-century Spain, herded into crowded ghettos across Europe, and were often, in the places they wound up, prevented from owning farmland. Thus Jewish literature talks about the cities Jews left, the harbors that received them, the new neighborhoods they hurriedly settled. Mountains, being places of repose, tend to get left out of this narrative.

Which is probably why I'd never heard the story of my paternal grandparents' forays into the Austrian mountains until recently, when I happened to read through a family history written by my grandfather Martin in 1979, two years after I was born, and a few years before he died.

My grandfather had arrived in Vienna from a small Polish village in 1917, at the age of seven, with his mother, brother, and three sisters. "It was not an easy trek," he wrote. "There were hay wagons and crowded trains, waiting and negotiations." The six of them had come to reunite with my grandfather's father, an alcohol dealer who had become stuck in Vienna during the First World War. They were a religious family, and in their new apartment in Vienna, a relative would come by regularly to teach my grandfather the Torah. The relative would often fall asleep in the middle of a lesson, and my grandfather would grab a preferred storybook, stashed nearby, and pull it into his lap.

In the summers, my grandfather swam in the Donau Canal, a detour of the Danube River. In the winters he skied in the Wienerwald, a section of the Austrian Alps that reaches into Vienna, using *goiserers*, hiking boots that strap onto skis.

Later, in Vienna, he met my grandmother and dreamed of taking her on a train trip to the Schneeburg, a mountain about forty miles from the city, where they would climb to the top and relax in an emergency shelter. Her mother, however, refused to give permission for such a trip if it involved an overnight. "There was no such thing as backtalk to one's parents," my grandfather wrote. So the couple began the trip at 3:00 a.m., climbed the mountain, warmed themselves in the shelter, descended, and got back to Vienna, "in time to satisfy my future mother-in-law."

It was a sweet, relatively easy time. But soon my family would be on the move again.

3. NUMBERS, 2006

New York, where my grandfather and grandmother ended up after barely escaping Hitler's Anschluss with their lives, is more than 4,000 miles west of Vienna. Seattle, where my parents arrived after fleeing the strictures of their East Coast upbringing, is, of course, much farther west—and much less Jewish. Here, I am forever floored by the number of people who remark on my being Jewish as if it were some very curious and foreign thing, but perhaps I shouldn't be surprised. There are about 37,000 Jews in greater Seattle, according to a "Jewish Census" commissioned in 2000 by the local Jewish Federation. If that number is still roughly accurate, then Jews currently make up less than one percent of Seattle's overall population.

By contrast, in Los Angeles, a 1997 survey found well over half a million Jews—a number roughly equivalent to the entire population of Seattle for that same year. In the San Francisco area, a 2004 study found more than 225,000 people living in Jewish households, making them 10 percent of that region's overall population. And in New York state, the world's biggest Jewish center outside of Israel, there are nearly two million Jews, with Jews in Manhattan making up about 12 percent of that borough's population.

I went to college in Manhattan, where meeting a Jew is like spotting a taxi. On the Upper West Side, where I was living, December would bring more apartment windows lit with electric menorahs than with Christmas lights. When I went out to bars with male friends who happened to be Jewish, no one ever assumed my Jewish friends must be related to me, as often happens here.

In Seattle, people tell me over and over that I'm the only Jew they know, which constantly amazes me. But, again, perhaps I shouldn't be surprised. The other night I was talking with a friend who said that before he temporarily left this city, at the age of eighteen, to attend college on the East Coast, he didn't know what a Jew was. Even more astounding: The number of Seattleites who know I'm Jewish and yet ask me, year after year, what I'm doing for Christmas.

There continues to be a basic and widespread ignorance in this city about some of the fundamental tenets of Judaism, an ignorance that is no doubt linked to the low number of Jews in this area, but one that continually leads to awkward encounters, annoying conversations, and embarrassingly ham-handed actions from public officials. Take, as one example of this region's bumbling dealings with Jews, the silly contretemps that erupted this year over the Christmas trees at Sea-Tac airport. The whole thing was absurd and dripped with a thinly veiled small-town longing for national attention (no matter that getting this national attention involved boarding the "War on Christmas" crazy train). But it was nevertheless telling that after Sea-Tac officials were confronted by a litigious rabbi who wanted a menorah on display at the airport in addition to the Christmas trees, the officials temporarily took down the trees and publicly admitted that they had never given any thought to their exclusively Chistmas-y decorations. This would be too embarrassing an admission to make in a more Jewish city. However, in a region that tends not to think much about Jews, it was accepted as an understandable oversight.

Similarly, last year, when a candidate for the board of the Seattle Monorail Project, Cindi Laws, suggested that her Jewish opponent was being financed by wealthy Jews in an alleged anti-Monorail Jewish conspiracy, her defense was largely the same—that she hadn't thought much about Jewish sensitivities until some vaguely anti-Semitic sentences came tumbling out of her mouth.

In the 2000 census by the Jewish Federation, 28 percent of Seattle-area respondents said they had personally experienced anti-Semitism in the past five years, and the most commonly reported experience was being singled out unfavorably in a social relationship. This doesn't surprise me. In Seattle, I haven't experienced anti-Semitism in the classic sense of being called a "kike" or checked for horns beneath my hair, or in any of its more violent manifestations, such as the shooting earlier this year at the Jewish Federation, in which Naveed Afzal Haq, a loner upset with Jews, killed Pamela Waechter, a fifty-eight-year-old Jewish fundraiser, and injured five other women. But I do frequently find myself in social situations where people say amazingly stupid things about me, or Jews in general. Often, I chalk it up to them never having known a Jew. But at times it can seem an almost willful ignorance, one that makes me wonder whether, at the root of this ignorance, there is some anti-Semitic disinterest, or perhaps disdain.

Lately, as Seattle becomes more sophisticated, and people here travel to and from bigger cities, where they learn that all the cool kids in the really big cities tend to be down with the Jews, I've been presented with a new type of awkward encounter. This one involves the Seattle hipster who wants to prove that he's so down with the Jews that he's able to make harsh fun of them, to their faces, in front of his friends. This is, of course, a variation on the white guy who wants to publicly call his black friend "my nigga," and sometimes, in the right room, in front of the right people, or with good friends, a certain amount of post-Jewish, post-anti-Semitic humor works. There is something liberating about being able to laugh at one's own identity, especially in the presence of people who don't share it. But the precondition for this is a shared understanding and respect for the identity that's being mocked. In Seattle, that precondition is rarely met. More often, I experience what happened to me at a party the other weekend: I walked up to the back stoop, where people were outside smoking, and a young hipster friend announced to the rest of the gathering that "the Jew" had arrived. Since it's not safe to assume any random gathering in Seattle is ready for post-anything jokes, all eyes turned to me, and I was expected to provide a cue, to either get upset or laugh, so that the rest of the gathering would know whether to be silently outraged (as is the Seattle way) or ironically amused (as is the Seattle hipster way).

I like to say nothing in these types of situations, and instead just stare at the eager-to-be-down hipster, trying to achieve an expression that can be interpreted as either annoyance or diffidence, one that lets everyone marinate in the real issue: their own clumsiness at dealing with Seattle's Jewish problem.

4. JUDE, 1938

I have a Jewish problem of my own. I'm not an extremely religious person. I celebrate the major holidays (Rosh Hashanah, Yom Kippur, Passover), but I do it less out of an articulable faith in a divine power than out of a limited respect for tradition, the enjoyment of certain rituals and the healthy social interactions they encourage, and, to be completely honest, a hedging of bets.

As a rule, I prefer rational thought to superstitious thought, but all my life I have been observing Yom Kippur, the holiday in which I atone for a year's worth of bad deeds, forgive those who have harmed me with their bad deeds, and in exchange, am supposedly written into the next year's "Book of Life" by God. I haven't died yet. Every year at Yom Kippur I think: Why stop observing now and tempt the easily angered deity of the Old Testament, if He indeed exists? In this same vein, I have developed a habit of silently saying the first among Hebrew prayers, the Sh'ma, upon takeoff and landing at airports. Again, I haven't died yet.

I bring all this up to explain my guilt. It is not about my failure to rise to the defense of my religion and the Hebrew God when people like the guy at the party do stupid things related to my being Jewish; I figure my own idiosyncratic version of Judaism, which people like the guy at the party don't understand anyway, is far more of a problem in the Hebrew God's eyes than my failure to throw cheap wine in the face of some overly cheeky acquaintance. What I feel guilty about relates to my grandfather. I feel that my grandfather Martin, who was rounded up by the Nazis, but through luck and connections managed to escape Austria in 1938 with "Jude" stamped in his passport, would not be amused at my tolerating the glib use of my Jewishness as a party punch line.

5. ISLANDS, 1902

The best-known wave of Jewish immigration to America, the one that is lodged in the popular consciousness, is the wave that brought my grandfather Martin to New York, the one that occurred in the 1930s and 1940s during the Holocaust. But it was much earlier waves of immigration — often occurring for similar reasons, such as pogroms in Eastern Europe or rising anti-Semitism in Turkey—that built Seattle's Jewish community. In 1910 there were 4,500 Jews in Seattle, and they made up a significantly higher percentage of the city's overall population (about 2 percent) than they do today.

In general, the Jews who landed in Seattle were people who had money to risk in starting a new business in a frontier town (like the German Schwabachers, successful businessmen from San Francisco who became some of the city's first lenders and grocery-store owners); people with a sentimental attachment to a geography of islands and water (like the two Jews from the Turkish island of Marmara who came here in 1902 with a Greek friend, felt at home, and sent for their relatives); people who had adventurous souls (like Adolph Friedman, the first Jew on record to set foot in Washington state); or people who already had relatives here (like the entire town of Skapiskis, in Lithuana, which seems to have followed a few relatives to Bellingham).

By contrast, the Jews who came to America during and immediately after World War II were desperate, many looking for the safety of a large Jewish community. Like my grandfather, they were for the most part happy just to have made it to New York. Of the 150,000 Jews who arrived in the U.S. in the 1930s and '40s fleeing Hitler's Germany, only 1,000 of them settled in Seattle.

The East Coast Jews of this period developed an identity formed by opposition. My grandfather Martin had known the worst of Europe's anti-Semitism. My other grandfather, William, was teased for his Jewishness growing up in 1920s Brooklyn, and, after graduating law school, had his career path curtailed by the anti-Semitism at major

New York law firms. The Jews of Seattle, for the most part, have had a different experience.

From the beginning, Jews here were part of the business and political elite. One of the first territorial governors in Washington, Edward S. Salomon, was Jewish. Seattle's sixth mayor, Bailey Gatzert, was a Jew from Mississippi (by way of Germany) who'd first been drawn to California by the gold rush, and then up to Seattle by his marriage into a family of West Coast Jewish merchants. He spoke English with a southern drawl, served as a Seattle City Council member for several terms, and when he died, in 1893, received an obituary in the *Seattle Post-Intelligencer* that began: "The history of Seattle can never be told without telling much of the life of Bailey Gatzert." When, in 1897, the steamer *Portland* landed at the Seattle waterfront bearing more than a ton of gold from Alaska and setting off the Northwest gold rush that would put Seattle on the map, the ship docked at a place named Schwabacher Wharf. And as Seattle subsequently boomed into a frontier town where eager prospectors bought equipment and passage to the Klondike gold fields, Jewish merchants often became richer than the prospectors themselves, selling pre-made packs of supplies and equipment designed to last a man a year in the Klondike. At Cooper & Levy Pioneer Outfitters, located at First Avenue and Yesler Way in what is now Pioneer Square (and what was then a neighborhood filled with actual pioneers), the packs of equipment were stacked along the sidewalk and sold, twenty-four hours a day, for $1,000 each.

These early Jewish merchants were generally part of the first wave of Jewish immigrants to Seattle — Jews of German descent. After the Germans, beginning in the 1880s, came Eastern European Jews, and then, just after the turn of the twentieth century, a wave of Mediterranean Jews. Although these Jews didn't face much organized anti-Semitism, they did, following a long and rich pattern of minority-group in-fighting, look down on one another. The German Jews, generally better educated and more assimilated, looked down on the Eastern European Jews, the newer arrivals. And the Eastern European Jews, in turn, looked down on the Mediterranean Jews, with their strange water pipes and unpronounceable dishes, like *borekas* (stuffed, savory pastries) and *ashuplados* (Passover meringues), which were definitely not traditional European Jewish staples like gefilte fish.

Part of this was a result of the long-standing division between Ashkenazic Jews (Jews from Eastern Europe) and Sephardic Jews (Jews from the Mediterranean and North Africa), a division likely rooted in European racism and the need of despised minorities to have someone else to despise, even if that means despising someone more similar to them than different. Thus, as recounted in the aptly named *Family of Strangers*, the Ashkenzic kids of Seattle called the Sephardic kids "Mazola," for the olive oil they used in their cooking, and the Sephardic kids called the Ashkenazic kids "schmaltz," for the chicken fat used in their food. But these divisions were also an outgrowth of the intense longing among Seattle Jews to assimilate; the fear behind much of the acrimony was that some Jews were making the rest of the Jews look bad.

All of which goes some way toward explaining another problem of the Jewish community in Seattle: Its sense of itself, which is thin and fractured.

There was a Jewish neighborhood that emerged in Seattle's Central District in the '20s, '30s, and '40s, and it had about it the flavor of the famous tenements of lower Manhattan during the same period—friends and relatives from the old country squeezing into small rented houses, Yiddish-speaking housewives bickering over chicken feet, a parade of dressed-up Jews moving up and down Yelser Way on the Sabbath, heading to and from temple (or synagogue, or, as the Russian Jews called it, shul). But this neighborhood didn't have quite the same crowded desperation or rivalry with other nearby immigrant groups that one would have found in New York, and it didn't have nearly the number of Jews; in fact, even in Seattle's "Jewish neighborhood," Jews were never a majority.

In addition, the local Jewish community lacked a strong artistic class to record the feeling of the time. There was no Saul Bellow of Seattle writing "I am an American," no Allen Ginsberg writing "when I was seven momma took me to Communist Cell meetings," no Gershwin writing musical scores that would later become soundtracks for movies written by some Seattle version of Woody Allen, no great Jewish painters or singers to speak of. And so there never developed a recognizable sense of the "Seattle Jew," as has developed in New York, Chicago, and L.A.—a Jew with a literature, a sound, a textural memory. The closest Seattle Jews came to artistic greatness was by familial association. Ferdinand Toklas, cofounder of Washington's first department store, was the father of Alice B. Toklas, the writer and partner of Gertrude Stein (both she and Stein made their mark elsewhere, however). In itself, that distant connection—more about a Seattle businessman than a true Seattle artist—is a metaphor for Seattle's Jews. To this day, though many prominent Seattle Jews are major benefactors to the arts (the Benaroyas, for example), this city's best-known Jews remain, as in the pioneer period, businessmen: Howard Schultz of Starbucks, Jeff Brotman of Costco, the downtown developer Martin Selig. To the extent that anti-Semitism lurks beneath the surface of some social interactions in the Northwest, it could be due, in part, to the one-dimensional (and stereotype-reinforcing) reputation of Seattle's better-known Jews: all of them powerful merchants or rich businessmen.

As for the Jews of the old Jewish neighborhood, without strong anti-Semitism to unite them in opposition, they lived together for a time and then, once they had established themselves, moved out of the Central District, surrendering it to Japanese immigrants and African Americans. The Sephardic Jews ended up in Seward Park where, as a proportion of this city's overall Jewish population, they now constitute one of the largest Sephardic communities in America. The Ashkenzic Jews moved to Capitol Hill, North Seattle, and, later, Mercer Island. Behind it all was an overwhelming drive to blend in. When certain clubs, like the Seattle Tennis Club and the Washington Athletic Club, banned Jews from membership, older establishment Jews who were allowed to remain on the rolls said nothing, kept their club privileges, and left the fighting to others.

These days, there is only one Jewish temple remaining in central Seattle, Temple De Hirsch Sinai, on Capitol Hill. The rest of the central Seattle synagogues have been transformed into something much different, like the old Bikur Cholim Synagogue at 17th Avenue and Yesler Way, which is now the Langston Hughes Cultural Arts Center. There, the decorative Jewish stars that were once carved into its façade and the engraving of the Ten Commandments that once inhabited the frieze over its entryway have long since been covered over with cement.

6. MEMORY, 2006

Aside from *Family of Strangers*, on which I relied heavily for this story, it wasn't easy to find source material for a piece about Seattle's Jews. There is no Jewish museum here, no central repository for a grand narrative about Jewish life in the Pacific Northwest. There are plans to create such a museum in Seattle, but they are nascent and at the moment moving rather slowly, especially for a community that has ample financial resources and a history that now goes back some 160 years in Washington state. Meanwhile, the local African-American community, which reached critical mass in Washington after World War II (several decades after the first big waves of Jewish immigration) is planning to open the Northwest African American Museum next year, inside the old Colman School in the Central District.

It may well be, however, that the local Jewish community has more pressing concerns than the creation of a museum. I am an anomaly among Seattle Jews in that I am, at least on my father's side, a third-generation American, carrying around with me the memory of my immigrant grandfather Martin. One of the major findings of the 2000 "Jewish Census" was that Seattle is the first-documented "fourth generation" Jewish community in the United States. "Most Seattle Jews, especially those under forty, have no direct connection to the immigrant experience and traditions through their own families," the report stated.

This is one of the most important of all local Jewish trends, because for more than a century the immigrant experience has been central to Jewish identity in America—first for the immigrants themselves, and then for the children and grandchildren of the immigrants, the generations that grew up in the presence of aging transplanted Jews, hearing Yiddish and rolling their eyes at their elders' foreign habits. My grandmother Frances spoke of an old-country way of making gefilte fish that involved a carp swimming around in a bathtub, and we all still laugh when someone brings up that messy-sounding endeavor. She is dead now, as are all but two of the older members of my family who were present, in 1977, in the house on the edge of the once-Jewish Central District, to watch my circumcision ceremony. Nora, my non-God-fearing godmother, is in her late seventies and still living in Vancouver. William, my Brooklyn-born grandfather, is ninety-one and now living at the Kline Galland Home for Jews in Seward Park, where matzoh ball soup appears to be on the menu every day.

Seattle, of course, is already a much different place than the Jewish Brooklyn of my grandfather's youth, and largely by design of Jews who came here precisely because they wanted to wear their Jewishness more lightly, or were born into this lightly Jewish community and now know nothing different. In Seattle, according to the "Jewish Census," more than half of all people who identify as Jewish have no formal ties to any synagogue or Jewish group. Of all local marriages entered into by Jews, about half of them are "intermarriages" to a partner who is not Jewish.

And according to the National Jewish Population Survey of 2000 to 2001, Jews in Western states such as this one are far more likely than Jews elsewhere in the country to tell demographers that they are neither orthodox, conservative, nor reform Jews, but rather "just Jewish" or "secular Jews."

The old notion of what it means to be Jewish is unraveling here in Seattle at the same time as the thread of the story of Washington Jewry is being dropped—or, if not completely dropped, then at least let very slack. When my grandfather William dies, there will be no more Yiddish speakers in my immediate family, but at least there will remain, on the East Coast, plenty of museums and other testaments to his experience, the experience of a first-generation Jewish American born to immigrants in 1915, the same year Bellow was "Chicago born."

There with my grandfather at the Kline Galland home in Seward Park, however, are other Jewish Americans, Seattle born, who remember the neighborhood on Yesler Way and the peculiar arc that Jewish identity has followed over the last century in this un-Jewish town. When they die, it's not clear how this city is going to tell their stories, or if it is even interested.

What do **Fawziya Farah's** *friends like most about her? "My personality," she says. Fawziya was born in Somalia and speaks Somali and English. Her father and mother inspire her, and she dreams of becoming a top model.*

MY SPECIAL BROTHER

FROM *Having Them Here...*

by Fawziya Farah

MY YOUNGER BROTHER Radwaan and I live in Seattle, Washington, where he was born and where it rains a lot. There are a lot of crazy people who walk around talking nonsense in downtown. Seattle is beautiful. For example, the Space Needle is big and colorful and if you go up to the top you can see everything.

I have the best brother in my whole family. My brother has the funniest personality. He would fall down on purpose just to make my sister and me laugh. My brother is two years old, with big, brown eyes and black hair. He has a strong head. He is chubby, and light-skinned. One day, I was mad at my sister for taking my favorite stuffed animal without asking me. My brother came and made everything better. He made me laugh so hard that I forgot what I was mad about. That's why I love my brother.

Radwaan is so special to me. I have two other brothers but I haven't seen the older one for a long time, and the younger one is eleven months old and kind of boring. My brother Radwaan can already speak two languages: English and Somali. Radwaan is a big help in my family. He loves his little brother and he is the second youngest in my family. I love Radwaan.

Tad Iritani, *who was ten when he wrote this story, would like the superhero ability to shape-shift so he could swim in the ocean and see fish.*

TAD THE SHAPE SHIFTER

FROM *What It Takes*

by Tad Iritani

MY NAME IS TAD. I am ten years old and I have the power to shape-shift into anything that I see. I live on Earth and I am deathly afraid of water. The thought of drowning is what makes me afraid of water. I don't know where this fear originated, but I have been afraid of water as long as I can remember.

Today I have to go fishing on Lake Bob and I am not very excited about it. I really wish that I didn't have to go. My brother Brandon was supposed to go but he says that he's "sick." In actuality, he just wants to stay home and watch the football game. My dad wants to go to catch northern pike and, apparently, he really needs my help.

As it seemed unavoidable, I went out on the boat. It wasn't long before my favorite toy, Mr. Ducky, fell out of the boat. The wind picked up and the water started to ripple. Mr. Ducky looked like he was surfing on waves as the water carried him away and out of reach. I was petrified and I didn't know what to do. I had to save Mr. Ducky because he actually generates all of my superpowers and without him I am nothing. I went over to my dad and told him I really needed the ducky. He said he had a fish on the line and couldn't turn the boat around. If I wanted Mr. Ducky then I would have to jump in and swim after him. We got in an argument because I was too afraid of the water to jump in.

Suddenly my inner soul kicked in, my legs started pumping, and I propelled myself off of the back of the boat. My heart was pumping rapidly as my skin hit the ice-cold water. I swam as fast as I could but soon realized I wasn't going anywhere because the current was against me. Actually, it was good because I could see Mr. Ducky being carried by the waves back towards me. I reached out for Mr. Ducky and just as I grasped him in my hand I felt something pull me under, deep into the water. My worst fears were coming true. I felt like I was drowning. I thought it must be an undercurrent pulling me down, but then I saw IT!

The face was horrifying—it was half northern pike and half piranha and he was mad! He was the one that my dad had on his fishing pole and he was fighting with all his might. I had heard about him—the "Bob Monster of Lake Bob," who weighed a ton and could eat people in a single bite. The fishing line was wrapped around my leg and keeping me under the water. I had to think quickly— then I remembered that I was holding Mr. Ducky and he could help me shape-shift. I saw a tadpole swimming by and shape-shifted into a tadpole with developed legs, so that I would be able to get out of the water if necessary. I quickly grabbed the fishing line and bit through it right above where it was wrapped around my leg. I sunk my teeth into the end of the fishing line and tugged with all of my might. I wanted my dad to keep reeling in the fishing line, so that he could reel me in.

Dad pulled up the fishing line, soon realizing that he had caught a tadpole. He was cussing until I shouted, "DAD," and he realized that it was me. When I saw my dad, I was able to shape-shift back into my human form. After this experience, I was thankful for my powers and even more afraid of the water.

Lauren Weedman *doesn't mean to brag, but her book* A Woman Trapped in a Woman's Body *was named by Kirkus Reviews as a Top 10 Indie Book for 2007. She is an award-winning solo theater performer and has worked in film and television, including being a correspondent on The Daily Show during the one year they didn't win an Emmy. When it's raining in the Northwest, her favorite place to be is steaming toward Orcas Island on a ferry.*

I SEE THE DOLPHINS!

by *Lauren Weedman*

On our lunch break during a rehearsal for "an irreverent musical comedy," all the other actors noticed Nick's head suddenly slump to his chest. Everyone thought he was nodding off. But I knew his hot wings had just arrived and he was saying grace.

At the cast party, Nick stood in the corner of the room, rocking back and forth. People assumed he was on something, but I could see he was singing. Once I shoved my way past all the ironic conversations I got close enough to hear what he was singing.

The Carpenters.

"Day after day… I face a world of strangers where I don't belong…" he sang.

"Me too," I thought.

"I am not that strong!" he wailed.

"Me neither," I mouthed.

After he missed the bus, he moved in, and thanks to the romance of unemployment, we spent every single moment together. And then one day after he'd spent hours sitting on the bluffs at Discovery Park writing poems to me and making sketches of my lips he leaned close my ear, gave it a little kiss, and whispered, "I'm trying to control my thoughts right now. I'm trying not to think about Satan. If you even think about him, he sees it as an invitation…but me saying his name right now is not an invitation—do you hear me—" Then he turned his head towards the sky and screamed "NOOOOOOO!" at the top of his lungs.

Satan really is powerful, because after he was mentioned I was never fully comfortable around Nick again. It suddenly dawned on me that no good relationship starts with telling your friends, "See that guy rocking back and forth in the corner? That's HIM!" But was he crazy or was he artsy and spiritual? Maybe Nick's theory about schizophrenics—that they're the sane ones and WE'RE the crazy ones—applied to him as well. Perhaps he was supposed to be MY GREATEST LESSON.

Nick was pretty consistent in his pattern of giving a little crazy quickly followed by big love. It's what kept me there. But then one day he mixed it up and decided to follow a little crazy with a full-on clown parade. I was lounging on our sad little futon in our studio apartment watching TV, and during the commercials staring out the sliding glass door, that was also our front door, at the traffic going by on Queen Anne Avenue. (Having a sliding glass door as a front door was wonderful for letting in extra light but frustrating when you're trying to stomp out of the house after a fight. "I'm outta here!" and "SLAM!" is just so much more effective than "I'm outta here!" and "Slllllllllllllllllide.")

As I watched what seemed to me to be a parade of

Suburu Outbacks drive by, Nick was in the middle of his favorite daytime activity: smoking and staring at me for hours like I was one of those Magic Eye posters that had a three-dimensional picture that would suddenly appear out of all the dots if you unfocused your eyes just right and stared at it without blinking for three hours. Nick was obsessed with those posters in the mall and could never get them to "work." All the mall teenagers around him would suddenly scream "Oh my god, a dolphin! I see it!" and Nick would stomp away, frustrated that he didn't have "the gift." Nick absolutely believed that if he could train himself to see the hidden images he'd be able see into other dimensions.

He'd been staring at me for going on two hours and the only thing he'd discovered was that from some angles I looked like his mother…and then like a man…then back to his mother.

Unfortunately, all my Seattle friends thought Nick was a magical genius. A friend of mine who makes frog puppets on Vashon told me, "It sounds to me like he just embarrasses you. And that's more your issue than his. Don't you think?" Then he made me watch while he danced around the woods with one of his puppets.

I needed the help of an outsider. Someone who wouldn't suggest that we dance with puppets in the woods to scare our pain away. Someone who would take one look at Nick and say "What are you doing? You wanna help crazy people, go volunteer. There's too much and there's too much, and he's just too much. You're top shelf, you deserve better."

I needed my old gay boyfriend from high school, Jon.

The morning of Jon's arrival Nick had really busted open the crazy chest and was letting the cuckoo fly. He told me that he was moving into his van that was parked in front of our Queen Anne apartment for a few days. Not to give Jon more room but because he wanted to practice being homeless so that if it ever happened to him (you mean WHEN not IF, I thought) it wouldn't be a shock. Unlike the homeless, though, he had the freedom to come in and out of the apartment to use the restroom and grab some ice cream sandwiches from the freezer.

I tapped on the back window of his van.

Tap tap.

"I'm going to pick up Jon, and then I'm taking him to Discovery Park for a hike," I said.

Nick's sleepy face appeared and he looked at me for a moment like he didn't recognize me. "It's me! It's your mom disguised as Satan!" I yelled through the window. He ignored my joke and put his lips up to the window, waiting for me to kiss him back through the glass.

"This side is dirtier — I'm just gonna wave," I said, and ran to my car.

The moment that Jon's plane arrived from Los Angeles I knew that his visit would be a turning point. Telling me how to live my life was one of Jon's favorite things to do. He'd been doing it since seventh grade. "You are not a soprano, you are an alto, and I want you to march up there and tell the director! Now!" Plus he was good with crazy and delusion — he'd lived in L.A. for fifteen years.

I didn't want Jon's trip to feel joyless, so I waited until we'd finished singing the entire *Ain't Misbehavin'* medley before I launched in.

"Jon, I've got some major stuff that I need to talk to you about."

He gasped.

"Oh my god, me too. Find a coffeeshop. Preferably a gay one. Quick."

Moments later we were sitting at Vivace's drinking gorgeous lattes and I started giving him some highlights from Nick's and my relationship. I told Jon how Nick's eyes had started to get all watery and crossed thanks to walking around with a Magic Eye book in front of his face, which once caused him to hand a bus driver a two-for-one Crazy Bread Coupon from Little Ceasar's Pizza instead of a dollar. Jon's only response was, "I love that he takes the bus… that's so spiritual."

I'd forgotten that Jon had seen a photo of Nick and declared him "the most beautiful man I've ever seen!" This was going to be harder than I thought.

So I told him about the horror that I'd felt when, in the middle of this sweet family-friendly video store down the street from us, the entire store was scarred for life by hearing Nick ask the store owner if he had any porno where the people were in loving relationships because he was tired of seeing women get disrespected. I tried to distract the mortified mothers by grabbing *The Secret of Roan Inish* — "Remember the magic? Jimmy!!" — but it didn't work.

"I think that's kind of cool," Jon said. "He's a feminist."

"No! No, he's not!" I screamed. "And he keeps the porno playing all the time because he thinks it's not offensive because they're real people. They're not real people! They're porno people acting like they're real people. I recognize them from other movies!"

Jon just laughed and got up to order a third latte.

What was going on? This wasn't some quirky anecdote!

Why didn't anybody seem to take Nick's behavior as seriously as I did? Had everyone grown so accustomed to my exaggerations and half-truths that now nobody believed me? Or worse, did everyone secretly believe that Nick was exactly what I deserved? That I'd found my soul mate? Why wasn't Jon telling me to "GET OUT! NOW!"? When a mutual friend once told us about how she was angry at her boyfriend for handing her a dozen roses on her birthday still wrapped in plastic, Jon had been so outraged he immediately started looking up Safe Houses for Battered Women in her area. "He's never heard of a vase?!" he'd screamed at her.

"Okay, I have to tell you something," Jon said. He got very serious. Finally. "Something huge that you need to hear."

Please, I thought. Because that's exactly what it's gonna take to get me out of this relationship—something huge. How do you break up with someone who you know already feels so rejected by the world—Day after day he faces a world of strangers where he don't belong, he is not that strong—How do you break up with someone so fragile just to save yourself?

"Aliens."

"What?" I asked.

"Aliens."

Aliens? Oh my god, I could have cried. I really hoped he meant the movie.

"I'm completely obsessed with aliens. I've been reading a book about alien abductions and it's amazing. There is so much that we don't know and they don't want us to know. But, Lauren, I want to get abducted. I really do. So what I do is every night before I go to bed I simple meditate and let them know…I'm ready."

In the past, Jon had talked about healing colors and the importance of feng shui-ing your soul but he'd never gone this far. Apparently I was just a magnet for crazy.

He talked for so long that I stopped listening and my eyes started to blur and unfocus.

And that's when it happened. Jon's face turned into a million tiny dots and I saw it. I didn't have to stay with Nick. It was that simple. Jon's alien talk had been exactly what I needed because it let me know that he was going to be no help whatsoever and I'd have to figure this out on my own.

I didn't have to stay with Nick. I shouldn't have to be constantly blurring my instinct in order to handle spending time with him.

The vision of me living alone—free and happy—came leaping out of Jon's face. And I think I saw a dolphin.

LAUREN WEEDMAN

I SEE THE DOLPHINS!

ACKNOWLEDGMENTS

A NUMBER OF THANK YOUS are in order. First: 826 Seattle has so much gratitude to Amazon.com, the online book (and other things) seller who started right here in the Pacific Northwest. It is our Amazon.com pals who have generously funded the initial printing of this book. They give us money and then we have big ideas.

The aforementioned big ideas are often the result of collaborations, and this is certainly the case here. Teri Hein (Executive Director of 826 Seattle) stole (as usual) a seed of this idea from 826 Valencia who has developed partnerships with two hotels in San Francisco who support literacy. Margot Kenly, a major 826 Seattle pal and woman of many ideas, suggested we make an anthology of student and adult writing. It was Kim Ricketts who, with her trademark boundless spirit, waved her hand in the air to be the hotel and bookstore connection. We added Bill Thorness in at the beginning because he is so smart about book project management and always so generous with his time. This project couldn't have happened without 826 Seattle design guru, Justin Allan, who raised his hand to design the book, and what you are holding is the result of his genius.

Thank you to all the authors, young and not as young, who have donated their stories. And thank you to the many 826 Seattle volunteers who worked one-on-one with the students to perfect their stories...and to Bill Thorness and Kjersti Egerdahl for lending their editing skills.

One hundred percent of the proceeds of this book go to further the work of 826 Seattle, which teaches children across the Northwest the essential skill of writing.

We would be remiss not to thank the many photographers whose keen eyes have put faces to the names: Bill Thorness photographed Tesla Kawakami (p. 14), Emily Paulsen (p. 44), Jake Lindsay (p. 64), Noah Sather (p. 88), Autumn Straker (p. 110), Bharti Kirchner (p. 136), baklava (p. 142), and David Gonzalez (p. 160). Dan Pelle captured Jess Walter (p. 20), David Guterson's (p. 58) photo was taken by Alan Berner, and Paul Hughes' (p. 98) by Randall Statler. Jon Allred snapped Isabel Canning (p. 122) and Tad Iritani (p. 268). Teri Hein (p. 146) was photographed by Susan Doupe, and Kathleen Alcalá (p. 162) by Jerry Bauer. Alex Allred put her much-beloved kitchen to good use and created and photographed Popover Pancakes (p. 158), Loretta's Buttermilk Pancakes with Wild Blackberries (p. 179) and Salmon with Grapes (p. 183). Jason Little photographed Myla Goldberg (p. 180). Mary Koruga photographed Mustafa Ahmed (p. 190) and Fawziya Farah (p. 264). Po Bronson's photograph (p. 194) was taken by Chris Hardy. Finally, Kelly O took Eli Sanders' (p. 244) photo.

Book cover images of *The Summerfolk* (p. 78) and *Andrew Henry's Meadow* (p. 79) are provided courtesy of San Juan Publishing Company and Doris Burn.

The Museum of History and Industry, Seattle was kind enough to provide the photographs of Royal Brougham (p. 101, MOHAI photo number 1986.5.5G.181.1 and p. 106, MOHAI photo number 1986.5.20087), and Elvis at the 1962 Century 21 Expo (p. 132, MOHAI photo number 1986.5.40806.2). These photos are part of the Seattle Post-Intelligencer Collection.

And while we are on the subject of photos, our thanks to the estate of Max R. Jensen and Jess Cliffe of vintageseattle.org for providing the cover photo.